Assessing virtual exchange in foreign language courses at tertiary level

Edited by Anna Czura and Melinda Dooly

Published by Research-publishing.net, a not-for-profit association
Contact: info@research-publishing.net

© 2022 by Editors (collective work)
© 2022 by Authors (individual work)

Assessing virtual exchange in foreign language courses at tertiary level
Edited by Anna Czura and Melinda Dooly

Publication date: 2022/09/12

Rights: the whole volume is published under the Attribution-NonCommercial-NoDerivatives International (CC BY-NC-ND) licence; **individual articles may have a different licence**. Under the CC BY-NC-ND licence, the volume is freely available online (https://doi.org/10.14705/rpnet.2022.59.9782383720102) for anybody to read, download, copy, and redistribute provided that the author(s), editorial team, and publisher are properly cited. Commercial use and derivative works are, however, not permitted.

Disclaimer: Research-publishing.net does not take any responsibility for the content of the pages written by the authors of this book. The authors have recognised that the work described was not published before, or that it was not under consideration for publication elsewhere. While the information in this book is believed to be true and accurate on the date of its going to press, neither the editorial team nor the publisher can accept any legal responsibility for any errors or omissions. The publisher makes no warranty, expressed or implied, with respect to the material contained herein. While Research-publishing.net is committed to publishing works of integrity, the words are the authors' alone.

Trademark notice: product or corporate names may be trademarks or registered trademarks, and are used only for identification and explanation without intent to infringe.

Copyrighted material: every effort has been made by the editorial team to trace copyright holders and to obtain their permission for the use of copyrighted material in this book. In the event of errors or omissions, please notify the publisher of any corrections that will need to be incorporated in future editions of this book.

Typeset by Research-publishing.net
Cover Layout by © 2022 Anna Czura
Cover photo © 2022 studioroman via Canva.com

ISBN13: 978-2-38372-010-2 (Ebook, PDF, colour)
ISBN13: 978-2-38372-011-9 (Ebook, EPUB, colour)
ISBN13: 978-2-38372-009-6 (Paperback - Print on demand, black and white)
Print on demand technology is a high-quality, innovative and ecological printing method; with which the book is never 'out of stock' or 'out of print'.

British Library Cataloguing-in-Publication Data.
A cataloguing record for this book is available from the British Library.

Legal deposit, France: Bibliothèque Nationale de France - Dépôt légal: septembre 2022.

Table of contents

v   Notes on contributors

ix   Acknowledgements

1   Introduction
Anna Czura and Melinda Dooly

Part 1. Assessment in virtual exchange: theoretical background and research findings

13   The evolution of virtual exchange and assessment practices
Melinda Dooly

29   Virtual exchange: issues in assessment design
Anna Czura

47   Assessment in virtual exchange: a summary of the ASSESSnet project
Anna Czura and Melinda Dooly

Part 2. Assessment tools in virtual exchange

65   Learners' diaries as a tool for teachers' assessment in teletandem
Suzi Marques Spatti Cavalari and Solange Aranha

79   Peer group mediation sessions as an assessment tool in teletandem
Anna-Katharina Elstermann

93   Peer assessment of process writing in a virtual exchange project
Anna Czura and Agnieszka M. Sendur

107   TEAMMATES in virtual exchange: tool and tips for peer assessment
Melinda Dooly

Part 3. Case studies at tertiary level

123   Is (inter)cultural competence accessible? Assessing for fluency
Grace Dolcini and Grit Matthias Phelps

Table of contents

135 Assessing intercultural learning in virtual exchange
Anastasia Izmaylova

147 Business communication skills through virtual exchange – a case study
Jean-François Vuylsteke

163 Assessment in the English for Academic Study Telecollaboration (EAST) project – a case study
Anna Rolińska and Anna Czura

177 Author index

Notes on contributors

Editors

Anna Czura is a researcher, academic teacher, and teacher trainer. Her research interests centre around language assessment, intercultural competence, learning mobility, virtual exchange, CLIL, and European language policy. She is an assistant professor in the Institute of English Studies at University of Wrocław, and a post-doctoral researcher and Marie Curie fellow (MSCA IF) at the Department of Language and Literature Education and Social Science Education of the Autonomous University of Barcelona. She is a member of GREIP: Grup de Recerca en Ensenyament i Interacció Plurilingües (Research Centre for Teaching and Plurilingual Interaction). She also acts as the Polish Ministry of Education expert who certifies published teaching materials for school use. Orcid ID: https://orcid.org/0000-0001-5234-6618

Melinda Dooly is Serra Húnter Full Professor, Chair in Technology-Enhanced Language and Intercultural Education in the Department of Language and Literature Education and Social Science Education at the Universitat Autònoma de Barcelona. Her principal research addresses technology-enhanced project-based language learning, intercultural communication, and 21st century competences in teacher education. She has published widely in international journals and authored chapters and books in this area of study. She is the former (and founding) editor of Bellaterra Journal of Teaching and Learning Language and Literature and co-editor of the book series Telecollaboration in Education (Peter Lang). She is lead researcher of GREIP: Grup de Recerca en Ensenyament i Interacció Plurilingües (Research Centre for Teaching and Plurilingual Interaction). Orcid ID: https://orcid.org/0000-0002-1478-4892

Authors

Solange Aranha is Associate Professor of English at UNESP (São Paulo State University), Department of Modern Languages. Her research focuses on issues related to telecollaborative teaching and learning, teletandem, ESP, EAP, and genres. She has authored many publications in various outlets. Her research is

Notes on contributors

granted by FAPESP (São Paulo Research Foundation). Dr Aranha is the leader of the Research Group InViTe (Intercâmbio Virtual e Teletandem: Línguas Estrangeiras para Todos). She is currently the Coordinator of Language and Literature Programme at IBILCE.

Suzi Marques Spatti Cavalari is Assistant Professor at São Paulo State University (UNESP) at São José do Rio Preto. She is a member of the Linguistic Studies Graduate Programme, in which she supervises research activities in the area of applied linguistics. Her research interests lie in telecollaborative language teaching and learning, autonomy, and (self-)assessment. She is a member of the Research Group InViTe (Intercâmbio Virtual e Teletandem: Línguas Estrangeiras para Todos). She is the coordinator of the teletandem laboratory in her institute.

Grace Dolcini joined the Fachsprachenzentrum at Bielefeld Universität in 2012 as an instructor and assumed the co-coordinator position for the English language in 2017. She holds a BS in environmental science from the University of San Francisco and a Masters in English Language from Bielefeld Universität. Her research interests include cultural communication, online communication, and sociolinguistics.

Anna-Katharina Elstermann is a translator, German as foreign language teacher, and learning/writing adviser at the Writing Centre at Goethe Universität Frankfurt, Germany. After graduating in applied linguistics and cultural studies from Johannes Gutenberg Universität Mainz, Germany, she worked for about ten years at Universidade Estadual Paulista in Brazil in German teacher training and within the Teletandem Brasil project. Her main research interests focus on learning and teaching foreign languages through telecollaboration, advising in language learning, and plurilingualism.

Anastasia Izmaylova is the Director of the Language Learning Centre at Grinnell College, where she works with faculty and students to promote and coordinate language and culture learning. In her research, Dr Izmaylova focuses on intercultural competence development, as well as the use of latest technology tools in language instruction.

Notes on contributors

Grit Matthias Phelps joined the Department of German Studies in 2008, after completing her degree in German as a foreign language, American, and Romance studies at the Friedrich-Schiller University in Jena, Germany. Her research and teaching interests include interactive use of the Internet in language teaching, cultural communication, foreign language acquisition and teaching, and language competencies for life-long learners.

Anna Rolińska is an English for academic purposes lecturer at the Glasgow School of Art, UK. She is responsible for designing, teaching, convening, and evaluating English provision in the International Foundation Programme as well as the School's bespoke pre-sessional English for the creative disciplines. Her research interests include academic literacies, use of educational technology, formation of learner identity and agency, creativity in academia, and the interplay between multimodality and academic discourse.

Agnieszka M. Sendur is assistant professor at the AFM Krakow University, Poland (Krakowska Akademia im. Andrzeja Frycza Modrzewskiego) and an ESP instructor, teacher trainer, examiner, and author of coursebooks and other teaching resources. She is currently Head of the Foreign Languages Centre and a faculty member in the Faculty of Psychology, Pedagogy, and Humanities. Her research interests and areas of expertise include language testing and assessment, languages for specific purposes, technology in foreign language teaching and learning, distance learning, and academic integrity.

Jean-François Vuylsteke is a passionate senior language lecturer with more than 30 years of teaching experience at Bachelor level at the École Pratique des Études Commerciales (Belgium) where he teaches business English and cross-cultural business management. He has developed numerous offline bilingual collaborative projects for the last 25 years, first with Belgian universities, then, shifting to online exchanges with international partners in the UK, US, Hungary, and Palestine. For the last two years, he has been an Erasmus+ Virtual Exchange Project trainee and co-organiser of transnational virtual exchange projects.

Acknowledgements

We would like to thank the research participants; the teachers, who in spite of the unprecedented teaching load in the midst of the pandemic, agreed to participate in the ASSESSnet project and share their knowledge and expertise. Dear authors of the chapters, we cannot thank you enough for your commitment and generosity in bringing in your experience, teaching resources, and models of assessment that you have developed and tested over the years in your virtual exchange projects. We are also grateful to the peer reviewers listed below for their invaluable support in providing feedback on the contributions.

- Solange Aranha, São Paulo State University, Brazil
- Maria Christoforou, Cyprus University of Technology, Cyprus
- Xavier Fontich, Universitat Autònoma de Barcelona, Spain
- Anastasia Izmaylova, Grinnell College, USA
- Anna Klimas, University of Wrocław, Poland
- Klaudia Kruszyńska, Universitat Autònoma de Barcelona, Spain
- Suzi Marques Spatti Cavalari, São Paulo State University, Brazil
- Anna Nicoloau, Cyprus University of Technology
- Trisha Thrasher, University of Illinois at Urbana Champaign, USA
- Aleksandra Więckowska, Technical University of Wrocław, Poland
- Xiaoting Yu, Universitat Autònoma de Barcelona, Spain

This project has received funding from the European Union's Horizon 2020 research and innovation programme under grant agreement No 845783.

Introduction

Anna Czura[1] and Melinda Dooly[2]

1. Virtual exchange

Virtual Exchange (VE) is understood in this volume as an educational programme that involves interaction and collaboration with peers from different locations, facilitated by means of online technology (Belz, 2003; O'Dowd & Dooly, 2020; O'Dowd & O'Rourke, 2019). Depending on the educational context, theoretical foundations and pedagogical underpinnings, such programmes have been dubbed as telecollaboration, eTandem, teletandem, online intercultural exchange, or collaborative online international learning. All these terms "highlight both the medium (virtual, online, digital, distance, global, networked) and the underlying purpose (exchange, intercultural, collaboration, learning)" (O'Dowd & Dooly, 2020, p. 262). In recent years, VE has emerged as the most commonly used term due to its strong presence in the subject literature (Dooly & Vinagre, 2021) and the importance attributed to this educational approach by "governmental bodies and inter-governmental bodies" (Dooly & O'Dowd, 2018, p. 15 – see Chapter 1 for more detailed discussion of approaches to VE). Whereas in this introduction, we use VE as an umbrella term, the authors of the individual chapters were free to use the term that they considered as most relevant in their educational context, and that best describes the objectives and the form of the online exchange their students were involved in.

Over the last 20 years, VE has become a valuable tool used in tertiary level education to facilitate internationalisation at home and internationalisation of the curriculum (cf. Jager et al., 2019) and allow for intercultural interaction

---

1. Universitat Autònoma de Barcelona, Barcelona, Spain; anna.czura@uwr.edu.pl; https://orcid.org/0000-0001-5234-6618

2. Universitat Autònoma de Barcelona, Spain; melindaann.dooly@uab.cat; https://orcid.org/0000-0002-1478-4892

How to cite: Czura, A., & Dooly, M. (2022). Introduction. In A. Czura & M. Dooly (Eds), *Assessing virtual exchange in foreign language courses at tertiary level* (pp. 1-10). Research-publishing.net. https://doi.org/10.14705/rpnet.2022.59.1406

to students who, for different reasons, cannot take part in study abroad programmes. In the context of foreign language learning, the research has tended to focus on investigating the impact of VE on different aspects of foreign language competences (O'Rourke, 2007), intercultural skills (Belz, 2002; Vogt, 2006), learner autonomy (Fuchs, Hauck, & Müller-Hartmann, 2012), and selected transversal skills (Vinagre, 2010). However, what stands out is the fact that, despite being perceived as one of the most difficult aspects of running a VE project (O'Dowd, 2013), assessment remains a severely underexplored topic in research and teacher training handbooks (Akiyama, 2014; Dooly & Vinagre, 2021).

2. The ASSESSnet project

The "ASSESSnet: Language assessment in virtual mobility initiatives at tertiary level – teachers' beliefs, practices and perceptions" project was carried out to fill in the research gap in the subject literature about assessment in VE environments and offer practical implications that would offer support to foreign language teachers in designing assessment procedures and tools. The ASSESSnet project (www.assessnet.site) was a two-year project (2019-2021) carried out as a part of Marie Skłodowska Curie Actions individual fellowship (MSCA IF) at the Autonomous University of Barcelona (UAB) by Anna Czura (researcher) and Melinda Dooly (supervisor), with the cooperation of the GREIP (Research Centre for Plurilingual Teaching and Interaction) research group.

More specifically, the project aimed to explore teachers' beliefs about the function of assessment in VE as well as to collect data on how teachers plan, design, and implement assessment in their projects. Through the compilation of data about assessment objectives, tools, and criteria, we were able to analyse the relationship between summative and formative approaches to assessment and the use of specific assessment tools. Given the interdisciplinary nature of VE projects, the study also focused on the content of assessment, i.e. the elements of learners' activities and performances that are typically subject to assessment (e.g. foreign language competence, digital literacy, intercultural competence, and transversal competences). The data was collected by means of both qualitative (interviews) and quantitative (questionnaires) tools, which were supplemented by the analysis of the course syllabi and other assessment-related documents. At every stage, the research in the ASSESSnet project was practically oriented and planned with a view to providing hands-on recommendations and strategies for class use. This volume as well as all the publications presenting the study outcomes are available open-access on our website: http://www.assessnet.site and through the UAB repository.

3. Overview of this volume

This volume is an important output of our project and a testimony of our practical approach as it consists of chapters in which the authors present real-life examples that illustrate effective efforts of planning and administering assessment in virtual projects in a wide variety of tertiary level contexts. We were further motivated by our conversations with the participants of our study. "Examples, examples, examples!" is an emblematic response to the question about the training needs the teachers considered as most pressing as regard assessment in VE. The teachers called for hands-on resources and descriptions of real-life case studies that describe successful approaches to assessments in different contexts. Upon being presented the idea for the volume and subsequently agreeing to contribute a chapter, one of the authors said: "this is exactly what I would have needed when I started".

This volume is our response to those entreaties. The authors describe assessment in VE courses that involved synchronous, asynchronous, or a mixture of these two communication approaches, and took place in settings in which the participation in a VE component was either an integral part of the syllabus or offered as a voluntary activity. In their chapters, the authors explain why they decided to choose specific assessment tools and how these were adopted to correspond with the institutional requirements, course objectives, and students' needs. The descriptions of assessment procedures are often complemented with

Introduction

concrete examples of task descriptions, assessment rubrics, self-assessment prompts, and examples of student outputs. In their chapters, the authors also share their reflections on the evolution of their approaches to assessment and the struggles they dealt with underway.

The ASSESSnet study indicates that assessment in VE is hugely diversified across contexts and we are fully aware that the assessment approaches presented in this volume may not find a straightforward application in other settings. Neither we nor the contributors to this volume had the goal of offering ready-made solutions because we are aware that all-fitting formulas are never possible in the teaching profession. However we can identify practical and effective examples that have been successfully tested in other settings that serve as examples for others for inspiration for their own contexts and teaching needs. This book is produced *by* practitioners *for* practitioners with the objective of facilitating future assessment practices in VE projects. Although all the case studies describe VE projects in foreign language courses at tertiary level, we hope that the teachers working at other levels of education and those teaching other content subjects will find the guidelines applicable also in their contexts. The need for approachable and established solutions to assessment in an online environment that make an active use of computer-mediated communication technology in the classroom has become even more pronounced by the Covid-19 pandemic. VE is not tantamount to distance education, but as these two pedagogies use similar tools and are interrelated on many levels; consequently, the ideas collected in this volume have the potential to inform the design of assessment tools also applicable in other computer-assisted language learning contexts. Finally, this volume may be of interest to school authorities and policy makers interested in introducing this form of learning or improving the quality of existing projects taking place in their educational centres.

Part I, *Assessment in virtual exchange – theoretical background and research findings*, discusses selected aspects of VE and assessment design in foreign language education and offers a summary of ASSESSnet project research findings accompanied with the most pressing recommendations.

In the first chapter, **Melinda Dooly** provides a brief overview of the terminology that has most commonly been used for these types of exchanges and describes how the available technology at the time has had an impact on the focus of research and practice of the exchanges. This is followed by a discussion of the importance of assessment in the overall pedagogical design of VE.

In the second chapter, **Anna Czura** discusses selected issues in assessment theory that inform assessment design in VE. In particular, the focus is placed on the role of selecting and defining the construct as a means of ensuring assessment validity. This chapter illustrates how the purpose and the envisaged consequences of assessment may affect the choice of assessment strategies and tools in VE. The chapter concludes with the discussion of the role of sociocultural factors in assessment that need to be taken into account in pedagogical initiatives involving participants from two or more distinctive educational contexts.

Anna Czura and **Melinda Dooly** summarise the main findings of the ASSESSnet project. Following a more detailed description of project objectives and research methodology, the presentation of the results focuses on the role of institutions in shaping assessment practices, the assessment tools used, and teachers' beliefs about assessment objectives and pedagogies. On the basis of the results, the authors underline the need for stronger institutional support in VE, including greater flexibility in course design, fuller recognition of teachers' and learners' time investment, and more opportunities of targeted teacher training initiatives.

The following chapters present case studies that outline the assessment procedures and specific tools that have been designed for and implemented in concrete VE projects. All the texts follow the same structure. The *introduction* presents the authors' mission statement and the theoretical approach(es) underpinning their assessment practices in VE. The following section provides an *overview of the VE project*, outlining its institutional context, course type and objectives, language(s) used, task types, and other information the author(s) considered relevant. In the section devoted to the *assessment in the*

Introduction

VE project, the authors provide details of the assessment process, describe the assessment tools used, and delineate the assessment criteria. In many chapters, these are supplemented with examples of authentic assessment tools, rubrics, examples of student work, and other relevant documents. In the *conclusions and lessons learnt*, the authors critically reflect on the assessment process, highlighting the strong points of the implemented assessment, pointing out important challenges, and indicating possible future developments. Some authors share a selection of *recommended readings* that include suggested publications, resources, and websites for further exploration on the subject. Finally, some chapters also contain *appendices* with authentic assessment rubrics, research instruments, and other documents used during VE projects.

The case studies grouped in Part II, *Assessment tools in virtual exchange*, focus on a specific assessment technique (e.g. learning diary, peer assessment, or mediating sessions in assessment) and suggest how these can be employed to assess precise facets (e.g. intercultural competence, different aspects of foreign language competence, and collaborative skills).

The chapter by **Suzi Marques Spatti Cavalari** and **Solange Aranha** is devoted to learning diaries in institutionally integrated teletandem, a bilingual model of VE implemented in Brazil. Learning diaries provide a platform for exchanging experiences about the learning incidents, linguistic aspects, and difficulties that arise during synchronous sessions with a VE partner. In their chapter, we learn how a learning diary is used as a tool for evaluating, reflecting, and discussing ongoing setbacks through diary entries, examples of student-teacher interactions, and instructors' practical recommendations.

Next, **Anna-Katharina Elstermann** presents another tool used to encourage reflection in the Teletandem Brasil project, specifically peer group mediation. During the mediating sessions, which take the form of regular meetings that follow bilingual exchanges, the students, with the instructor's support, discuss how the new experience of taking part in VE has contributed to their language and intercultural and collaborative learning. The chapter provides hands-on guidelines on how to organise and facilitate mediating sessions, which prove crucial for challenging stereotypes and prejudices about the foreign culture.

The next two chapters concentrate on peer assessment in VE. Grounded on the critical reflection of previous VE projects involving students of tourism-related programmes, **Anna Czura** and **Agnieszka M. Sendur** designed a step-by-step procedure of introducing peer assessment in a task-based VE course involving three partner institutions. The evaluation criteria of the collaborative written task involved not only language accuracy and range, but also the use of appropriate rhetorical strategies and persuasive discourse. The chapter showcases the importance of scaffolding and synchronous feedback sessions in a course that centres on the process approach to writing and involves several rounds of peer assessment.

In her chapter, **Melinda Dooly** demonstrates how continuous peer assessment in VE can be supported by an online platform called TEAMMATES. The author guides us through the functionality of the platform that enables teachers and students to provide both numerical and open-ended feedback on other students' work. Receiving confidential observations from other team members allows the teacher insight into the functioning of the group work and the quality of team members' collaborative engagement. The chapter ends with underscoring the importance of adaptation measures, ongoing support, and open dialogue in helping students adapt to more autonomous learning and accept continuous peer evaluations as a valuable, and not anxiety-inducing, tool for assessing and learning in education.

Part III, *Case studies at tertiary level,* guides us through the entire assessment processes, offering insight into the assessment in different VE settings.

Grace Dolcini and **Grit Matthias Phelps** underline that assessment in VE needs to embrace the new role of language, which is not limited to grammar and vocabulary, but becomes a tool of intercultural communication. The chapter renders a course design in which course objectives and assessment are closely

Introduction

integrated and focus on different skills of interaction and skills of interpreting or relating. The assessment criteria in their fluency-oriented VE programme focus not only on the students' ability to communicate in a variety of situations, but also on their intercultural awareness and openness to new ideas and viewpoints.

Anastasia Izmaylova presents a two-sided approach to assessing student learning in a VE project, which consists in (1) formally assessing students' work and assigning a grade for their engagement in the tasks, including a portfolio; and (2) attending to students' intercultural competence development. It is explained how the initial assessment process had to be revised as the VE progressed, due to the limitations posed by the affordances of the online communication. The author explains how she approached assessing this complex construct in her research project by first singling out selected components and then applying a combination of elicitation tools, including a portfolio, questionnaires, and interviews. The chapter concludes with a reflection on how the research findings can find application in VE courses.

In the text describing his approach to assessment in a business English course combining foreign language communication and business skills**, Jean-François Vuylsteke** underlines the essential link between curriculum design, course objectives, and assessment in VE courses. The elaborate assessment system in this project comprises collaborative writing, peer and self-assessment, face-to-face conferences with the instructor, and additional feedback from an external professional recruiter. Given the complexity of the assessment process, the author underlines the importance of thorough planning and a transparent division of tasks between the involved agents. This helped to attain synergy in the assessment procedures applied in the two partner institutions, which, due to distinctive curricular standards, differed in terms of some tasks and grading policy.

In contrast, the next chapter presents an assessment procedure in a project in which there was a significant imbalance in students' roles between the partner institutions. **Anna Rolińska** and **Anna Czura** give an account of how assessment was approached by the UK partner in the English for Academic Study Telecollaboration project between science, engineering, and technology students. Whereas for the Palestinian students the involvement in VE was voluntary, for the UK-based students the project was a part of a high stakes course that played a decisive role in the university admission process. The text outlines how the instructors in the UK institution applied content-based assessment, which entailed a written report and oral presentation based on a discipline-related technological problem in the partners' context. The chapter also addresses the imbalances in the treatment of the participants as regards the assessment and feedback provision and suggests how these inequalities could be reduced in future VE projects.

As it has already been pointed out earlier in this text, VE has been widely reported to have a positive impact on students' personal growth, to help produce positive gains in foreign language competences, and to support development of intercultural and transversal skills. These case studies demonstrate the key role that assessment holds in the overall design of successful exchanges. The chapters also underscore that this is an area of study that has received less attention than other teaching and learning aspects of VE. It is our hope that this edited volume helps advance general knowledge of this vital aspect for teaching and learning languages (and other content matter) in geographically-distributed partnerships.

References

Akiyama, Y. (2014). Review of issues and potential solutions of Japan-U.S. Telecollaboration: from the program coordinator's viewpoint. *Studies in Japanese Language Education, 11*, 3-14.

Belz, J. A. (2002). Social dimensions of telecollaborative foreign language study. *Language Learning & Technology, 6*(1), 60-81.

Belz, J. A. (2003). Linguistic perspectives on the development of intercultural competence in telecollaboration. *Language Learning & Technology, 7*(2), 68-99.

Dooly, M., & O'Dowd, R. (2018). Telecollaboration in the foreign language classroom: a review of its origins and its application to language teaching practices. In M. Dooly & R. O'Dowd (Eds), *In this together: teachers' experiences with transnational, telecollaborative language learning projects* (pp. 11–34). Peter Lang.

Dooly, M., & Vinagre, M. (2021). Research into practice: virtual exchange in language teaching and learning. *Language Teaching*, 1-15. https://doi.org/10.1017/S0261444821000069

Fuchs, C., Hauck, M., & Müller-Hartmann, A. (2012). Promoting learner autonomy through multiliteracy skills development in cross-institutional exchanges. *Language Learning & Technology, 16*(3), 82-102.

Jager, S., Nissen, E., Helm, F., Baroni, A., & Rousset, I. (2019) *Virtual exchange as innovative practice across Europe*. Awareness and Use in Higher Education. https://evolve-erasmus.eu/wpcontent/uploads/2019/03/Baseline-study-report-Final_Published_Incl_Survey.pdf

O'Dowd, R. (2013).Telecollaborative networks in university higher education: overcoming barriers to integration. *Internet and Higher Education, 18*, 47-53. https://doi.org/10.1016/j.iheduc.2013.02.001

O'Dowd, R., & Dooly, M. (2020). Intercultural communicative competence through telecollaboration and virtual exchange. In J. Jackson (Ed.), *The Routledge handbook of language and intercultural communication* (2nd ed., pp. 361-375). Routledge. https://doi.org/10.4324/9781003036210-28

O'Dowd, R., & O'Rourke, B. (2019). New developments in virtual exchange for foreign language education. *Language Learning & Technology, 23*(3), 1-7. http://hdl.handle.net/10125/44690

O'Rourke, B. (2007). Models of telecollaboration (1): eTandem. In R. O'Dowd (Ed.), *Online intercultural exchange: an introduction for foreign language teachers* (pp. 41-61). Multilingual Matters. https://doi.org/10.21832/9781847690104-005

Vinagre, M. (2010). *Teoría y práctica del aprendizaje colaborativo asistido por ordenador*. Síntesis.

Vogt, K. (2006). Can you measure attitudinal factors in intercultural communication? Tracing the development of attitudes in e-mail projects. *ReCALL, 18*(2), 153-173. https://doi.org/10.1017/S095834400600022X

Part 1.
Assessment in virtual exchange: theoretical background and research findings

1. The evolution of virtual exchange and assessment practices

Melinda Dooly[1]

Abstract

This chapter provides a general synopsis of the evolution of Virtual Exchange (VE) as it has progressively become more immersed in the paradigms of language teaching approaches. Inevitably, this transformation unfolds in pace to advances in communication technology as the interactional tools are key for facilitating connection between distanced partners in the exchanges. Coming full circle, these advances have had an impact on the organization of the exchanges as well as the focus, methods, and tools used for assessing VE. We will first foreground seminal authors' work and their impact on VE, next we will review the more commonplace terminology and how these terms have evolved. Through this lens we will then consider how, historically, these concepts have impacted and are now manifested in the different typologies of implementations and assessments in more current VE research and practice, including the chapters in this book. We finish by presenting some of the thornier challenges in assessing VE and examples of how these are being addressed.

Keywords: virtual exchange, assessment, online interaction, intercultural teaching.

---

1. Universitat Autònoma de Barcelona, Spain; melindaann.dooly@uab.cat; https://orcid.org/0000-0002-1478-4892

How to cite: Dooly, M. (2022). The evolution of virtual exchange and assessment practices. In A. Czura & M. Dooly (Eds), *Assessing virtual exchange in foreign language courses at tertiary level* (pp. 13-27). Research-publishing.net. https://doi.org/10.14705/rpnet.2022.59.1407

Chapter 1

1. Introduction

Increasingly sophisticated technology has become ubiquitous in many households around the world; smartphones are now widely used around the world (although, admittedly there are still glaring socioeconomic gaps in places without electricity that makes the use of technology impossible). However, as technological advances and access to technology becomes more widespread, it is often argued that these events hold the potential to revolutionize teaching and learning. This was made patently palpable during the school lockdowns precipitated by the Covid 19 pandemic. Recent studies show that the situation activated teachers to develop and enhance their techno-pedagogical know-how and gain confidence in their technological abilities as the pandemic led to the shutting down of schools for extended periods and teachers had to pivot almost immediately from in-person teaching to online.

However, there is a need to push beyond these parameters of merely thinking about technical teacher know-how; this does not guarantee true innovation in pedagogy. As Hodges et al. (2020) point out, a distinction is best made between techno-pedagogical competences and *emergency* remote teaching. As the use of technology in education has become more widespread, concomitantly and with increased access to personal digital devices and Internet connection, discussion of preparing the '21st century citizen', capable of functioning in a technology-saturated society, had already become prevalent in discourse on education and educational policies even before the worldwide pandemic. One of the most common features for '21st century education' is that the leading-edge teacher should use student-centered, inquiry-based teaching approaches – the same characteristics asserted by Dewey (1916) 100 years ago in his proposal for a transformative educational model. In his framework, Dewey argued that the role of education is to provide *developmental opportunities* for the individual (guidance and support to knowledge, not transmission from one 'all-knowing' to 'empty vessels'). Significantly, from 2020 to 2021, during the most critical moments of the Covid pandemic, numerous policy support documents for educators in online teaching also tended to highlight student-centered practice. Significantly, this shift from a "transmission mode of pedagogy" to a more "participative experience" (Thomas, Reinders, & Warschauer, 2013, p. 7) had already been the backbone of learning design for VE for several decades (Belz, 2003; Dooly, 2005, 2009; O'Dowd & Waire, 2009; Warschauer, 1996).

A second major axis of 21st century, participatory education, which is the rejection of the notion of 'individual cognition' for a more collaborative process of socially constructed, mutually shared knowledge building has also been increasingly more predominant in VE configurations (Dooly, 2017). Social constructivists view knowing as a social process, manifest not only in the sociocultural construct of what is perceived as 'knowing' (Maturana, 1978; Mercer & Sams, 2006), but also within the social interaction among experts-to-non-experts, peer-to-peer that leads to higher levels of reasoning and learning (Sfard & Kieran, 2001). Therein lies another fundamental parallelism to the promotion of VE for learning. It has been well-documented that collaboration in education, whether between, classmates, entire classes or school and even between educational institutions and other entities or communities is not a new activity (Dooly, 2017; Dooly & O'Dowd, 2018; The EVALUATE Group, 2019). However, VE, as a specific type of collaboration that involves distanced partners has became more popular with the advent and easier access to communication technology in the late 1980s and early to mid-1990s, in particular in language education. This is not surprising as "fomenting contact between language communities has always been a principal goal (as witnessed by international programs of exchange, e.g. Erasmus programs)" (Dooly, 2017, p. 169) and with increasingly easier access to speakers of different languages, the use of VE is still growing.

2. Definition(s) of VE

This increment in the use of VE, concurrent with the rise of distanced online learning has led to some debate regarding what exactly comprises a VE. As researchers and practitioners' interest in VE has grown, several definitions – spanning decades – have been suggested.

Chapter 1

> "[VE], Telecollaboration, eTandem or Teletandem and Collaborative Online International Learning (COIL) are some of the more well-known terms that have been used, often interchangeably, to refer to the process of communicating and collaboratively learning with peers from different locations through the use of technology. Admittedly these terms are not considered by everyone to be synonyms and each term has emerged from different epistemologies and contexts. Moreover, the terms, if seen differently (some researchers do claim they are synonymous) are not mutually exclusive, and arguments regarding differences in terminology are often linked to an individual's dynamics and background references" (Dooly & Vinagre, 2021, pp. 1-2).

Some terminology – and authors most frequently associated with these terms – have had significant impact in *defining and describing* these types of exchanges, as seen in Figure 1. The key words used in the definitions also demonstrate significant evolution in the *focus* of the exchanges.

Figure 1. Evolution of keyword

(Mostly) asynchronous connections	(Mostly) synchronous connections	Mobile devices, broadband ...
Virtual connections	Social interaction Dialogue Debate Intercultural	VE Teachers Innovation Linguistic, intercultural & digital competences
1995	1996 2003	2016 2020
	Learning Languages & cultures (of the other)	VE/COIL Tasks Partner classes Teacher guidance

In 1996, Warschauer referred to technology-enhanced exchanges as 'virtual connections'. A year later, Little and Brammerts (1996) described tandem learning as a partnership between people with different mother tongues working together to learn each other's language and learn about each other's character and culture. In 2003, Belz used the term 'telecollaboration' for internationally distanced language classes that use Internet communication tools "to support social interaction, dialogue, debate, and intercultural exchange" (p. 2). In 2016, O'Dowd and Lewis place telecollaboration, VE, and online intercultural exchange on the same spectrum, explaining that all three terms refer to engaging students in task-based interaction and collaborative exchange projects under the guidance of their teachers. In 2020, the EU Commission stated that VE can help teachers to shift from their accustomed teaching approaches in order to develop new skills to engage in linguistic, intercultural, and digital learning experiences. In 2021, Dooly and Vinagre describe how VE is increasingly used by institutions and governments, arguing that the phrase VE "appears to be set as the most recognizable term, at least in the EU and the USA, although admittedly in South America [...] teletandem is a more predominant term" (Dooly & Vinagre, 2021, pp. 2-3). The evolution of the terminology applied to these contexts, as well as the expansion of overall goals – and subsequent complexity of design of VE – can also be perceived in the chapters in this book. Cavalari and Aranha (2022) use several terms to describe their exchange: teletandem (a common term in South America, in particular in Brazil), telecollaboration, and VE.

Moreover, as interest and research in these types of exchanges has extended from small pockets of pioneering practices to institutionally-based innovation (The EVALUATE Group, 2019), VE is increasingly considered a teaching approach, in particular in language education and under the larger paradigm of the communicative approach (Dooly & Vinagre, 2021). Subsequently, the EU (2020) is now calling for 'VE teacher competences'.

With VE progressively acknowledged as a teaching approach, a list of commonalities have been identified: (1) it is a highly flexible teaching practice; (2) it ensures opportunities for social interaction and collaboration with other learners outside formal classroom boundaries (pluriculturality); (3) it can be an alternative to physical mobility for students; and (4) it may include some self-directed learning within an array of institutionally planned learning activities (adapted from Dooly & Vinagre, 2021). It is important to note that neither individual, self-guided learning, nor one-teacher per class distanced, online learning constitute VE because, by default, it comprises teacher-supported collaboration between *at least two* partner classes in different locations.

Figure 2. Toward VE as an established language and intercultural teaching approach

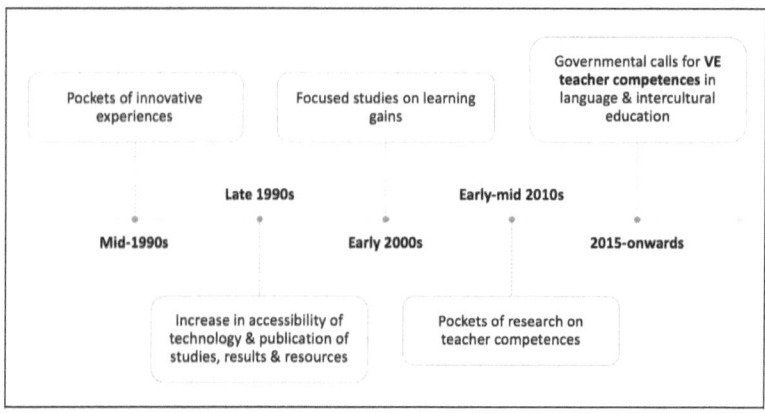

As mentioned in Dooly (2017), the above-described evolution of how VE is conceived also demonstrates that the use of digital exchanges in educational settings has gone from rather simple activities, largely viewed as complementary tasks, to far more complex, embedded, and holistic components of "learning ecologies" (Barron, 2006, p. 195). The main features of these definitions and foci, in particular collaborative learning, are also evident in the ways in which VE has been identified across the span of this book. Vuylsteke (2022, this volume) explains how two international business course students "worked collaboratively in order to develop both their digital and language skills" so that the learners could "keep learning when outside the classroom [… through …] peer-to-peer learning" (pp. 148-149). Czura and Sendur (2022, this volume) state that "one of the defining features of VE is collaboration, which involves working with other peers both from the home and the partner institutions, toward a common goal" (pp. 93-94).

The increasing complexity of VE is also evident in the chapters in this book. Cavalari and Aranha (2022, this volume) foreground both the task design and the relevance of learner interaction: "telecollaboration involves different pedagogical tasks by means of which students should learn and co-construct knowledge" (p. 66). For Rolińska and Czura (2022, this volume) the deployment of project-based learning in VEs can help bring authenticity and hands-on learning to the exchange.

The break from more formal classroom boundaries, in order to bring in a more pluricultural focus of language teaching and learning is also prevalent in the chapters in this book. Izmaylova (2022, this volume) emphasizes the "goal of providing students with an opportunity to analyze their own and target cultures, as well as practice their intercultural communication skills" (p. 136), just as Dolcini and Matthias Phelps (2022, this volume) highlight the relevance of intercultural competence gains that can come about through VE. Similarly, Rolińska and Czura (2022, this volume) describe how the learners "work across borders and cultures on real-life [disciplinary] scenarios and develop a number of soft skills and attributes alongside" (p. 163).

The aforementioned aspect of an incremental focus on self-directed learning is a transversal theme through several of the chapters. Dooly (2022, this volume) focuses principally on the notion of small working groups, meeting outside of class time without teacher presence; accentuating the need for increased learner autonomy in the overall process of VE. Elstermann (2022, this volume) highlights autonomous foreign language learning; self-directed learning can be facilitated through opportunities for working collaboratively with others around the world as key goals for VE.

Nonetheless, the amount, intensity, and format of collaboration in VE is not a settled debate as of yet, in particular if it is a component to be evaluated. The model below, proposed to preservice teachers involved in VE (Dooly & Sadler, 2020), provides a simple yet functional measurement tool for deciding and designing the type of collaboration between VE partners (informally called the 'Collaborate-o-meter').

Chapter 1

Figure 3. Collaborate-o-meter

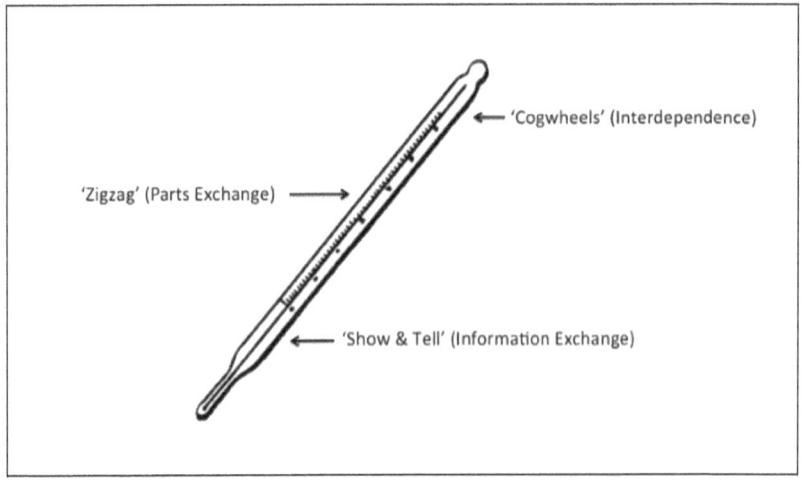

Cogwheels (interdependence): This is the hardest type of project to design and implement but it is the most rewarding. It involves complete interdependence between the online partners.	Zig-zag (parts exchange): This type of activity may involve group work in the local classes so that the learners can prepare something (information, key features of the output, etc.) to share with the other class. Each partner is responsible for part of the project output.	Show & Tell (information exchange): Probably one of the more common types of telecollaborative exchanges, this usually involves introductions, information about schools, communities, countries, hobbies, etc. There is language practice, but collaborative learning is minimal.

3. Shifting paradigms of VE and assessment

As described earlier and seen in the chapters in this book, the general underlying paradigm of VE has moved more and more to embrace and bring to the fore an emphasis on situated, learner-centered social practices, based on influential thinkers like Vygotsky (1930-1934/1978), Wertsch (1985), and Tharp and Gallimore (1988), to name a few of the more celebrated theorists in educational circles in the 1980's. There is now a widely accepted premise of VE that the teacher is a knowledge facilitator (Doolittle & Hicks, 2003; Dooly, 2017; Fosnot, 2005; Thomas et al., 2013) who designs and implements an optimal environment for learners to construct knowledge through engagement with 'artifacts', aided by expert and peer interaction (Chaiklin, 2004; Vygotsky, 1978).

Inevitably, the heightened focus on learner autonomy, peer assessment, and social interaction for collaborative learning has also had an impact on how assessment is conceptualized and applied to VE. All teachers must make decisions about assessment that acknowledges and appreciates the differences between the teacher's expectations and beliefs about learning compared with those of the students. For instance, while historically in many cultures cheating has often been understood to mean the illicit use of information or improper access to answers, this idea of cheating needs to be re-examined in the light of the underlying paradigms of VE.

If the focus of the exchange is on collaboration, VE teachers must think about using innovative assessment methods that move away from the notion of individual knowledge and instead focus on multiply-shared knowledge construction that is prevalent in online communities, facilitated through digital communication tools (Dooly & Sadler, 2013).

Assessment design that involves peer feedback and evaluations, as outlined by Czura and Sendur (2022, this volume), Dooly (2022, this volume), and Elstermann (2022, this volume), not only matches the assessment procedures to the learning design, it also explicitly acknowledges and makes visible the value of peer learning to the students involved in the VE.

Communicative competence gains must also be seen as part of the interactional process, and assessed accordingly, rather than as a one-time, decontextualized 'recall' of discrete linguistic items. This premise can be identified in the assessment practice outlined in Vuylsteke (2022, this volume), where the learners are assessed at the end of their VE through the use of a 'realistic online job interview'. Contextualized assessment practices such as these also advance ideas on how to counteract what Hall, Cheng, and Carlson (2006) have asserted as an underlying theoretical flaw in much second language acquisition research, that is the assumption of homogeneity of language knowledge across *speakers and contexts* (p. 220). As stated in Dooly (2011), these authors contend that speakers' language knowledge should not be considered as homogeneous, nor "composed of a-contextual, stable system components" (Hall et al., 2006, p. 230). In other words, VE assessment should stem from the notion that an individual's use of language is not static, levels of accuracy and fluency will vary according to everyday contexts. A person writing a chapter for a book is far more likely to be punctilious and aim for precise language use in comparison to when she is quickly texting an SMS message to a friend or colleague. Awareness of variants in contextualized language use can be accommodated through formative assessment, as discussed in Cavalari and Aranha's (2022, this volume) use of learner diaries or in Rolińska and Czura's (2022, this volume) description of periodically submitted output and 'bespoke feedback' criteria.

Another commonplace challenge for assessment of VE is how to extricate Intercultural Competences (IC) from technological abilities; 'cyberspace' is not culture-free and technical issues (expertise versus non-expertise) or technological discomfiture (lack of digital know-how) can transfer into attitudes toward the exchange (dislike of the imposition of doing VE as part of the academic work for instance) as well as having an impact on others' interpretation of an individual's response (for instance, out-of-screen distractions in the local environment can give the impression of being disengaged in the task when, in reality, this may not be the case). The use of portfolios, as described in Izmaylova (2022, this volume), can provide detailed insight into each individual's development (process) through analytical snapshots of specific moments (products), while allowing for the non-linear fashion in which IC evolves in each individual. Portfolios also provide more leeway regarding momentary lapses in engagement caused by external factors as well as venues for personal explanations of behaviors seen negatively by peers (Dooly & Sadler, 2020).

Differing institutional and course demands, unequal access to technology, unsymmetrical command of the language of the exchange and other similar individual aspects can have impact on VE process and outcomes (missed deadlines, quality of the assignments), eventually leading to obstacles in the interpersonal relationships of the participants (Dooly & Vinagre, 2021). Dialogic reflection between teacher and learner, based on diary entries like the ones described by Izmaylova (2022, this volume) can help participants comprehend the multi-layered aspects of digital communication and overcome some of these barriers.

4. Conclusions

As in any classroom setting, one of the most difficult tasks for the teacher is designing assessment that reliably reflects what each individual student, each starting from different epistemic status, has gained during the learning activity. It has been argued that the most authentic assessment practices are integral parts of the curriculum and instruction process; that they serve to not only measure what has been learned but also to support the learning during the process while facilitating a gradual increase in learner accountability for the process (Dann, 2014). Along these lines, VE assessment activities will ideally make a positive impact on students beyond certifying their knowledge gains and levels of competence, while advancing their learning capabilities beyond the VE experience. The chapters herein lay the groundwork for pushing forward new ideas for VE practitioners as well providing some useful insights for future research and practice.

References

Barron, B. (2006). Interest and self-sustained learning as catalysts of development: a learning ecology perspective. *Human Development, 49*, 193-224. https://doi.org/10.1159/000094368

Belz, J. A. (2003). From the special issue editor. *Language Learning & Technology, 7*(2), 2-5. https://doi.org/10125/25193

Cavalari, S., & Aranha, S. (2022). Learners' diaries as a tool for teachers' assessment in teletandem. In A. Czura & M. Dooly (Eds), *Assessing virtual exchange in foreign language courses at tertiary level* (pp. 65-78). Research-publishing.net. https://doi.org/10.14705/rpnet.2022.59.1410

Chaiklin, S. (2004). The zone of proximal development in Vygotsky's analysis of learning and instruction. In A. Kozulin, B. Gindis, V. S. Ageyev & S. M. Miller (Eds), *Vygotsky's educational theory in* cultural context (pp. 39-64). Cambridge University Press. https://doi.org/10.1017/CBO9780511840975.004

Czura, A., & Sendur, A. M. (2022). Peer assessment of process writing in a virtual exchange project. In A. Czura & M. Dooly (Eds), *Assessing virtual exchange in foreign language courses at tertiary level* (pp. 93-106). Research-publishing.net. https://doi.org/10.14705/rpnet.2022.59.1412

Dann, R. (2014). Assessment as learning: blurring the boundaries of assessment and learning for theory, policy and practice. *Assessment in Education: Principles, Policy & Practice, 21*(2), 149-166. https://10.1080/0969594X.2014.898128

Dewey, J. (1916). *Democracy and education: an introduction to the philosophy of education.* MacMillan.

Dolcini, G., & Matthias Phelps, G. (2022). Is (inter)cultural competence accessible? Assessing for fluency. In A. Czura & M. Dooly (Eds), *Assessing virtual exchange in foreign language courses at tertiary level* (pp. 123-134). Research-publishing.net. https://doi.org/10.14705/rpnet.2022.59.1414

Doolittle, P. E., & Hicks, D. E. (2003). Constructivism as a theoretical foundation for the use of technology in social studies. *Theory and Research in Social Education, 31*(1), 71-103. https://doi.org/10.1080/00933104.2003.10473216

Dooly, M. (2005). Working with an educational portal: a first-timer's experience. *TESOL-Spain Newsletter, 29*, 18-19.

Dooly, M. (2009). New competencies in a new era? Examining the impact of a teacher training project. *ReCALL, 21*(3), 352-369. https://doi.org/10.1017/S0958344009990085

Dooly, M. (2011). Divergent perceptions of tellecollaborative language learning tasks: task-as-workplan vs. task-as-process. *Language Learning & Technology, 15*(2), 69-91. https://doi.org/10125/44252

Dooly, M. (2017). Telecollaboration. In C. Chapelle & S. Sauro (Eds), *The handbook of technology in second language teaching and learning* (pp. 169-183). Wiley-Blackwell. https://doi.org/10.1002/9781118914069.ch12

Dooly, M. (2022). TEAMMATES in virtual exchange: tool and tips for peer assessment. In A. Czura & M. Dooly (Eds), *Assessing virtual exchange in foreign language courses at tertiary level* (pp. 107-120). Research-publishing.net. https://doi.org/10.14705/rpnet.2022.59.1413

Dooly, M., & O'Dowd, R. (2018). Telecollaboration in the foreign language classroom: a review of its origins and its application to language teaching practices. In M. Dooly & R. O'Dowd (Eds), *In this together: teachers' experiences with transnational, telecollaborative language learning projects*. Peter Lang.

Dooly, M., & Sadler, R. (2013). Filling in the gaps: linking theory and practice through telecollaboration in teacher education. *ReCALL, 25*(1), 4-29. https://doi.org/10.1017/S0958344012000237

Dooly, M., & Sadler, R. (2020). "If you don't improve, what's the point?" Investigating the impact of a "flipped" online exchange in teacher education. *ReCALL, 32*(1), 4-24. https://doi.org/10.1017/S0958344019000107

Dooly, M., & Vinagre, M. (2021). Research into practice: virtual exchange in language teaching and learning. *Language Teaching*, 1-15. https://doi.org/10.1017/S0261444821000069

Elstermann, A.-K. (2022). Peer group mediation sessions as an assessment tool in teletandem. In A. Czura & M. Dooly (Eds), *Assessing virtual exchange in foreign language courses at tertiary level* (pp. 79-91). Research-publishing.net. https://doi.org/10.14705/rpnet.2022.59.1411

EU. (2020). *Staff working document on the digital education action plan*. European Commission.

Fosnot, C. T. (2005). (Ed.). *Constructivism: theory, perspectives, and practice* (2nd ed.). Teachers College, Columbia University.

Hall, J. K., Cheng, A., & Carlson, M. T. (2006). Reconceptualizing multicompetence as a theory of language knowledge. *Applied Linguistics, 27*(2), 220-240. https://doi.org/10.1093/applin/aml013

Hodges, C., Moore, S., Lockee, B., Trust, T., & Bond, A. (2020). The difference between emergency remote teaching and online learning. *Educause Review, 27 March*. https://er.educause.edu/articles/2020/3/the-difference-between-emergency-remote-teaching-and-online-learning

Izmaylova, A. (2022). Assessing intercultural learning in virtual exchange. In A. Czura & M. Dooly (Eds), *Assessing virtual exchange in foreign language courses at tertiary level* (pp. 135-146). Research-publishing.net. https://doi.org/10.14705/rpnet.2022.59.1415

Little, D., & Brammerts, H. (1996). (Eds). A guide to language learning in tandem via the Internet. *CLCS Occasional Paper No. 46.* Centre for Language and Communication Studies, Trinity College.

Maturana, H. R. (1978). Biology of language: the epistemology of reality. In G. A. Miller & E. Lenneberg (Eds), *Psychology and biology of language and thought* (pp. 27-63). Academic Press.

Mercer, N., & Sams, C. (2006). Teaching children how to use language to solve maths problems. *Language and Education, 20*(6), 507-528. https://doi.org/10.2167/le678.0

O'Dowd, R., & Lewis, T. (2016). (Eds). *Online intercultural exchange: policy, pedagogy, practice. Routledge Studies in Language and Intercultural Communication.* Routledge.

O'Dowd, R., & Waire, P. (2009). Critical issues in telecollaborative task design. *Computer Assisted Language Learning, 22*(2), 173-188. https://doi.org/10.1080/09588220902778369

Rolińska, A., & Czura, A. (2022). Assessment in the English for Academic Study Telecollaboration (EAST) project – a case study. In A. Czura & M. Dooly (Eds), *Assessing virtual exchange in foreign language courses at tertiary level* (pp. 163-175). Research-publishing.net. https://doi.org/10.14705/rpnet.2022.59.1417

Sfard, A., & Kieran, C. (2001). Cognition as communication: rethinking learning-by-talking through multi-faceted analysis of students' mathematical interactions. *Mind, Culture, and Activity, 8*(1), 42-76. https://doi.org/10.1207/S15327884MCA0801_04

Tharp, R. G., & Gallimore, R. (1988). *Rousing minds to life: teaching, learning, and schooling in social context.* Cambridge University Press.

The EVALUATE Group. (2019). *Evaluating the impact of virtual exchange on initial teacher education: a European policy experiment.* Research-publishing.net. https://doi.org/10.14705/rpnet.2019.29.9782490057337

Thomas, M., Reinders, H., & Warschauer, M. (2013). Contemporary computer-assisted language learning: the role of digital media and incremental change. In M. Thomas, H. Reinders & M. Warschauer (Eds), *Contemporary computer-assisted language learning* (pp. 1-12). Bloomsbury.

Vuylsteke, J.-F. (2022). Business communication skills through virtual exchange – a case study. In A. Czura & M. Dooly (Eds), *Assessing virtual exchange in foreign language courses at tertiary level* (pp. 147-162). Research-publishing.net. https://doi.org/10.14705/rpnet.2022.59.1416

Vygotsky, L. S. (1978). *Mind in society: the development of higher psychological processes* (M. Cole, V. John-Steiner, S. Scribner & E. Souberman., Eds.) (A. R. Luria, M. Lopez-Morillas & M. Cole [with J. V. Wertsch], Trans.) Harvard University Press. (Original manuscripts [ca. 1930-1934])

Warschauer, M. (1996). (Ed.). *Telecollaboration in foreign language learning*. University of Hawai'i Second Language Teaching and Curriculum Center.

Wertsch, J. V. (1985). *Vygotsky and the social formation of mind*. Harvard University Press.

2. Virtual exchange: issues in assessment design

Anna Czura[1]

Abstract

Virtual Exchange (VE) is typically set up in an institutional context, which implies the need to verify student learning through assessment. The difficulties in designing and implementing assessment in VE arise principally from the complexity of VE itself, as well as from a combination of institutional and sociocultural factors. This chapter aims to discuss the main tenets that need to be considered when designing assessment in VE on tertiary level. In particular, the importance of defining the construct and selecting appropriate content in safeguarding the validity of assessment is highlighted. The chapter also discusses the interplay between the purposes and the consequences of assessment in VE, and the form of assessment. All of these features are interconnected and often need to compromise formative and summative functions in order to comply with the institutional requirements. Next, the constructive alignment between the course objective, learning tasks, and assessment is addressed. The chapter concludes with the discussion of the sociocultural factors that require particular consideration in pedagogical initiatives involving participants from two or more distinctive educational contexts.

Keywords: virtual exchange, assessment, validity, constructive alignment.

---

1. Universitat Autònoma de Barcelona, Barcelona, Spain; anna.czura@uwr.edu.pl; https://orcid.org/0000-0001-5234-6618

How to cite: Czura, A. (2022). Virtual exchange: issues in assessment design. In A. Czura & M. Dooly (Eds), *Assessing virtual exchange in foreign language courses at tertiary level* (pp. 29-45). Research-publishing.net. https://doi.org/10.14705/rpnet.2022.59.1408

Chapter 2

1. Introduction

By definition, VE is a learning programme "set up in an institutional context" (Helm, 2013, p. 28; Dooly, 2022, this volume), which implies that the students carry out assigned tasks to achieve concrete learning outcomes specified in the course description. Within institutional parameters, normally, students' time and work investment is expected to be assessed – to verify the fulfilment of the learning objectives, to offer students corrective feedback, to help teachers reflect on the effectiveness of their own work, and to provide the institution and funding bodies with evidence of learning (see more about assessment accountability in e.g. McNamara & Roever, 2006; Miller, 1999). However, the results of a recent European project indicate that as many as 36% of teachers do not assess students learning in VE in language learning contexts (Guth, Helm, & O'Dowd, 2012). Additionally, there is a shortage of research studies, practical resources and training opportunities that tackle this important aspect of running VE (Akiyama, 2014; Dooly & Vinagre, 2021).

The difficulties in designing and implementing assessment in VE arise principally from the complexity of VE itself, as well as from a combination of institutional and sociocultural factors. First of all, VE is considered to be the most complex and unpredictable of computer assisted language learning pedagogies (Kurek, 2015; O'Dowd, 2013). Kurek (2015) considers VE to be a complex learning environment, in which many individual agents constantly interact, influence, and depend on one another. In VE, the main axis consisting of teachers, students (in all participating institutions), and technology is supplemented with "the dynamic (and thus unpredictable) interplay of geographical distance of participants and their resulting cultural and linguistic diversity, married to double technology and language mediation, collaborative format, as well participants' different linguistic and cultural backgrounds" (Kurek, 2015, p. 18).

As regards evaluation in exchanges, this chapter sets out to discuss the main tenets that need to be considered when designing assessment in foreign language courses involving a VE component on tertiary level. First, the role of defining the construct and selecting appropriate content in ensuring validity is highlighted. The chapter presents how the purpose and the consequences of assessment administered in a higher education context may affect the choice of assessment methods and tools used in VE. Next, the constructive alignment between the course objective, learning tasks, and assessment is addressed. The chapter concludes with the discussion of the interplay between the above-mentioned elements of assessment design and the sociocultural factors that require particular consideration in pedagogical initiatives like VE, which involve participants from two or more educational contexts in different locations.

2. Issues in assessment design

2.1. Construct and content of assessment

The most important criterion of good assessment is validity (e.g. Brown & Abeywickrama, 2010; Messick, 1989). Assessment is valid when it assesses what it claims and intends to assess. To ensure validity, the first step in designing both the whole assessment strategy and a single assessment tool is identifying the construct, that is, the set of knowledge, skills, and abilities that a teacher intends to evaluate.

Thus, the construct of assessment is tightly linked to the course objectives and content; consequently, in the process of designing course assessment, teachers and other stakeholders involved need to ask themselves: *What knowledge/ skills or abilities does the course aim to develop?* In a foreign language course, depending on the course objectives, the construct may involve general foreign language proficiency or, more likely, achievement in listening, reading, writing, or speaking skills. Once the construct is identified, it is then necessary to determine what each particular item entails. For instance, students' writing skills in an essay assignment is typically broken down into several subcomponents (such as language accuracy, richness of vocabulary, and grammar structures, content and text organisation) and then described in detail in a rubric.

Even though on the surface level the main aim of VE in a foreign language course may seem to be the development of communicative competence, these complex projects support "a wide range of skills, knowledge, and behaviours" (Lee & Sauro, 2021, p. 34), which may include intercultural competence, content-related knowledge, and digital literacies (e.g. EVOLVE Project, 2020). To this, one can add 21st century skills such as collaboration, tolerance, critical thinking, problem-solving, leadership, and flexibility, which are inherent to intercultural VE projects that involve students engaged in completing a task-based activity (e.g. Helm & van der Velden, 2019; Mont & Masats, 2018).

Designing assessment rubrics may be a daunting task that often involves thorough literature review in search for the most appropriate theoretical model. Izmaylova (2022, this volume) describes the process of designing tools and criteria that aimed at assessing intercultural competence for research and pedagogical purposes. Teachers involved in VE can design such criteria on their own, adapt rubrics prepared by other practitioners, or refer to established reference documents that offer descriptors of selected competences and skills. For instance, O'Dowd (2010, p. 352) presents a sample assessment rubric for marking a blog in VE that consists of such criteria as structure and organisation, languages and communication, intercultural and sociolinguistic aspects, and online literacies.

All the reference tools described below, available online free of charge, may help teachers design their own rubrics describing selected competences gained during VE. The Common European Framework of Reference – Companion Volume (CEFR CV, Council of Europe, 2020) offers updated lists of descriptors for language competences and activities, as well as descriptors for mediation, online interaction, and plurilingual/pluricultural competence. Along similar lines, FREPA[2] (Candelier et al., 2007), a reference document for pluralistic approaches, presents a comprehensive list of descriptors of knowledge, skills, and attitudes that underpin plurilingual and intercultural education. The assessment of intercultural skills can be also supported by the framework of the INCA Project (2004), which consists of an array of assessment instruments,

---

2. A Framework of Reference for Pluralistic Approaches to languages and cultures: competences and resources

including a portfolio designed to assess intercultural competence, language, and subject knowledge competence. The Open Virtual Mobility[3] project targets skills and competencies obtained during virtual mobility, which apart from working in virtual teams, also embrace participation in online courses and internships. The outputs of this EU-funded project include an online self-assessment tool that enables students to reflect on their own virtual mobility skills in eight areas:

- intercultural skills and attitudes;
- interactive and collaborative learning in an authentic international environment;
- autonomy-driven learning;
- networked learning;
- media and digital literacy;
- active self-regulated learning skills;
- open-mindedness; and
- gaining knowledge of virtual mobility and open education.

The self-assessment tool is available in the Open Virtual Mobility Learning Hub upon login.

Having selected and clearly defined the construct, it is essential to make sure that the assessees' "performance on the assessment will really require the targeted knowledge, skills, or abilities and that the balance made between components in the assessment will provide a sound basis for the specific decisions that will be made about the assessees" (Green, 2014, p. 78). In other words, assessment should be designed in such a way as to reflect the range of knowledge, skills, or abilities discussed and developed during a particular course in order to provide students with sufficient feedback about their strong and weak points in each area. Such assessment should also offer teachers ample evidence to inform ongoing course modifications and future instructional planning. Figure 1 illustrates how the distribution of skills and abilities to be covered in a potential VE course should also be reflected in its assessment. Correspondingly, assessment should

---

3. https://www.openvirtualmobility.eu/

not address knowledge and skills that have not been covered in the course. For instance, the objectives of the hypothetical course exemplified in Figure 1 do not include the development of listening comprehension; consequently, the assessment of this skill in this particular course would yield invalid results and would fail to reflect students' efforts.

Figure 1. Illustration of content validity in course coverage and assessment coverage in a sample VE course

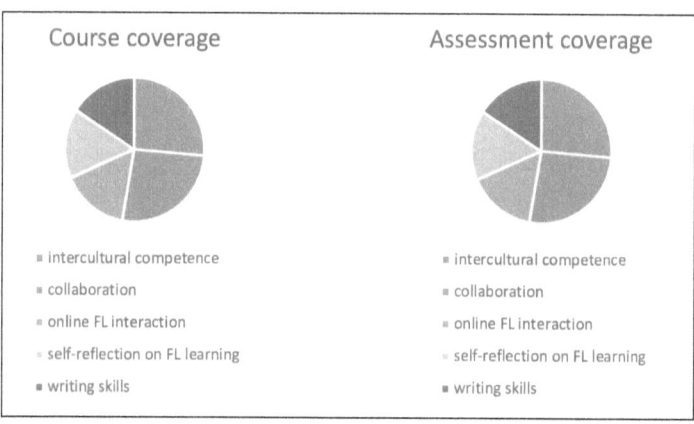

Dooly and Vinagre (2021) note that it "is not uncommon to read publications of VE that describe a predominantly oral modality for the learner interaction which is then assessed through a written essay of personal reflection of the experience" (p. 5). A possible solution involves assessing as wide a range of content as possible, on multiple occasions and by means of different forms of assessment – both formative and summative. This way, assessment targets different aspects of student learning throughout the whole course and yields more reliable and comprehensive feedback.

2.2. The purpose and consequences of assessment

Another question that needs answering is about the *purpose* of assessment in a given course. In classroom-based and VE contexts, the teachers most often employ the so-called achievement assessment, which "measure[s] learners' ability within a classroom lesson, a unit, or even an entire curriculum" (Brown & Abeywickrama, 2010, p. 9). Such curriculum- or syllabus-based assessment aims to observe students' progress and verify whether or not the learning objectives have been achieved within a particular course. Achievement assessment provides students with information of how much knowledge and competence they have mastered, and what areas require further improvement. As can be seen, being directly related to the course syllabus and content, this type of assessment is closer to the learners' experiences and therefore its aims and results are easier to understand and relate to. The teachers, on the other hand, receive valuable feedback on learners' progress, which supports instructional planning and allows for necessary modifications in the teaching approach and/or content. However, in some courses, teachers may prefer to apply proficiency assessment to establish students' overall level of specific knowledge or competences.

The further choice of assessment tools and procedures within the formative and summative assessment paradigm is closely linked to the *consequences* that assessment and its results may have for the learners. High-stakes assessment involves important consequences that may affect the learners' future, for instance grade promotion or graduation; whereas low-stake assessment typically consists of ongoing progress checks during a course. At tertiary level, the institution, by determining the stakes of assessment in a given course, has an impact on the shape and form of assessment in VE projects, its perceived importance, and the grading policy. Whether or not the students are awarded grades or credit points for their involvement in VE has an impact on their engagement, level of participation, and commitment to the task (Cloke, 2010; Rolińska & Czura, 2022, this volume).

Additionally, digital badges (or open badges) are gaining in popularity as a means of recognition of students' completion of tasks in VE projects. Digital badges are awarded on the basis of clear standards and criteria to certify that students have developed certain knowledge, skills, and achievements as a result of participating in a certain activity. For instance, students can present such

Chapter 2

online badges as evidence of skills and competencies developed during VE to apply for a scholarship or employment (for more detailed information about open badges see Hauck & MacKinnon, 2016; MacKinnon, Ensor, Kleban, & Trégoat, 2020). The idea of digital badges has been further supported by the European Commission's Erasmus+ VE project[4], during which these digital certificates were awarded to students, educators, and youth workers to certify their participation in project activities.

2.3. Approaches to assessment

The purpose and the consequences of assessment entail concrete instructional choices. In order to review what a student has learned during a course and represent it in the form of a grade or other evaluative standard, teachers tend to employ *summative assessment*. The obtained results are often used to report on students' progress and the effectiveness of the teaching process. On the other hand, when the direct purpose of assessment is to improve the quality of learning and teaching, *formative assessment* comes into play. Formative assessment, often termed as assessment *for* learning (Black et al., 2004; Black & Wiliam, 1998), as opposed to assessment *of* learning in the case of summative assessment, implies "the provision of information (usually in the form of feedback) to the learner in a form that the learner can use to extend and improve their own learning" (Hamp-Lyons, 2016, p. 21). There is a shift in the purpose of assessment – from "score reporting, certification, and creating league tables" (Hamp-Lyons, 2016, p. 22) to more learner-centred assessment, where the primary focus is placed on promoting students' learning and growth. The key element is the delivery of comprehensive and timely feedback that emphasises both positive and negative aspects of students' work with an eye to helping them improve their performance on an ongoing basis.

Summative assessment is typically associated with traditional tests, whereas such tools as portfolio, learning diary, and peer and self-assessment are considered inherent elements of the formative repertoire. However, the distinction between

---

4. https://europa.eu/youth/erasmusvirtual/erasmus-virtual-exchange-badges_en

these two types of assessment do not lie as much in the choice of specific assessment tools as in their purpose. There have been attempts to implement more formative tools, e.g. portfolio (Koretz, Stecher, Klein, & McCaffrey, 1994) and other means of self-assessment (Engelhardt & Pfingsthorn, 2013; Harlen & James, 1997) aimed towards more summative ends. Consequently, summative and formative assessment need not occur as a dichotomy, but as a continuum.

The ability to balance formative and summative purposes of assessment should be seen as an important element of teacher assessment literacy in VE. Continuous and formative assessment shows significant potential in VE contexts (Dooly, 2008) – it is integrated with the ongoing class activities, supports students' self-reflection, and facilitates the teaching process. In practice, however, teachers are often obliged to award students grades or other evaluative scores at the end of the course to meet institutional regulations and standards. As Huerta-Macias (1995) underlines, the "trustworthiness of a measure consists of its credibility and auditability" (p. 10). Thus, more alternative forms of assessment can also be used for summative purposes provided that "consistency is ensured by the auditability of the procedure (leaving evidence of decision making processes), by using multiple tasks, by training judges to use clear criteria, and by triangulating any decision making process with varied sources of data" (Huerta-Macias, 1995, p. 10). As mentioned earlier, for assessment to be valid, it needs to embrace all knowledge, skills, and abilities that have been covered in the course. This can be achieved by using an array of assessment techniques that cover different areas of student knowledge. Assessing student learning on multiple occasions throughout the course by means of different tools gives a more comprehensive and reliable picture of students' outcomes, strengths, and weaknesses. It also minimises the risk that a student's personal preference or learning style will affect the final outcome or grade – there are students who excel in collaborative tasks, whereas others are more disposed towards reflective and individual work.

Another approach to assessment of significant importance in the context of VE is task-based (language) assessment. The pedagogical design of a VE is recommended to be built around specific tasks (Dooly & O'Dowd, 2012;

O'Dowd & Ware, 2009), which are understood here as activities "in which a person engages in order to attain an objective, and which necessitates the use of language" (Van den Branden, 2006, p. 4). In VE projects, students often complete tasks in collaboration with their partners – they may co-design a brochure or a poster, write a CV, prepare a report, co-design a marketing strategy, etc. Such a task-based approach to class design should essentially find reflection in assessment. In Task-Based Language Assessment (TBLA), "tasks are used to elicit language to reflect the kind of real world activities learners will be expected to perform, and in which the focus is on interpreting the learners' abilities to use language to perform such tasks in the real world" (Wigglesworth, 2008, p. 112). Norris (2009) points out to three main functions of focusing on task performance in assessment: (1) it provides both the students and the teachers with formative and diagnostic feedback; (2) supports summative assessment of target language learning outcomes; and (3) sensitises students and other stakeholders to the communicative aim of language learning. Depending on the course objectives and criteria used, teachers may approach assessing students' performance in two ways.

> "In the 'strong' sense, assessment is made on the basis of the extent to which the actual task itself has been achieved, with language being the means for fulfilling the task requirements rather than an end in itself. In the 'weak' sense, the focus of the assessment is less on the task and more on the language produced by the candidate, with the task serving only as the medium through which the language is elicited – successful performance of the task itself is not the focus of the assessment" (McNamara, 1996, in Wigglesworth, 2008, p. 113).

The undeniable value of using tasks in assessment in VE is that they facilitate students' authentic language use in communicative situations that are likely to take part in outside of the classroom. TBLA can also be easily integrated into the ongoing course instructions and, what is more, promotes collaborative task completion, which is of central interest in a VE context. On the other hand, this form of assessment tends to generate a heavy workload on the part of the teacher and the students. Additionally, since task completion may involve a wide array of skills and competences, to ensure the provision of precise and targeted feedback, TBLA needs to be based on a set of clearly defined assessment criteria.

2.4. Constructive alignment

Constructive alignment (see Figure 2) is an approach to curriculum planning and delivery proposed by Biggs (1999), which assumes that learning outcomes, teaching, and learning activities and assessment need to be closely correlated in order to ensure high quality teaching and learning. Thus, irrespective of the subject matter and the mode of learning (in-class, online, or blended), it is prerogative that assessment be integrated in instructional planning. Moreover, the details of assessment – its objectives, tools, and criteria – should be aligned with the course learning outcomes, tasks, and teaching materials. Careful planning appears of crucial importance in VE, where the successful execution of the three elements presented in Figure 2 depend on close cooperation between the partner teachers and the participating institutions.

Figure 2. Constructive alignment (adapted from Biggs, 1999)

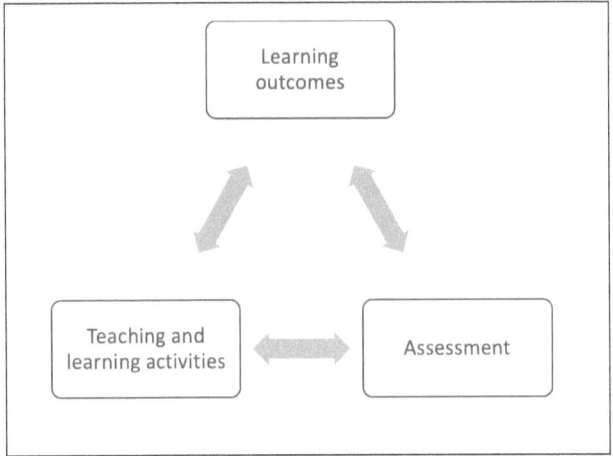

Gallagher (2017) underscores the dual role of feedback within this scheme: "feedback, and in particular formative feedback, provides ongoing opportunities for teachers and students to monitor the extent of the alignment of the existing three elements of the constructive alignment model" (p. 3011). This shared understanding of the link between course objectives, the tasks, and the assessment, with ongoing formative feedback as an integral part of instruction, supports teachers in instructional planning and, at the same time, gives students a sense of coherence and safety. Students are familiar with transparent course objectives and can expect that the assessment, both formative and summative, of their learning will reflect the envisaged learning outcomes, course content, and instructional methods they experienced throughout a given course.

2.5. Assessment as a social activity

Assessment should essentially be understood as a social activity because it is conditioned by the sociocultural contexts in which it occurs. To choose one example, language education policy has a direct impact on the content and the shape of classroom assessment as it determines "which language(s) should be taught, when (at what age), for how long (number of years and hours of study), by whom (who is qualified to teach), for whom (who is entitled and/or obligated to learn), and how (which teaching methods, curriculum, materials, tests to be used)" (Shohamy, 2007, p. 119). Furthermore, the impact of the educational policy and assessment stakes is also mediated by an interplay of more covert variables such as teachers' beliefs and professional development, and "traditional beliefs about teaching, learning, and assessment [that] dominate the learning community or culture" (Tierney, 2006, p. 258; also in Lock & Munby, 2000). Both the teachers' and students' perceptions of the role of assessment, the importance of constructive feedback, and their readiness for autonomous language learning and teaching (Lin & Reinders, 2019) may affect the latter's motivation, interest in the assignment, and, consequently, commitment and performance (McMillan & Workman, 1998).

There are additional complications in VE assessment. In VE we deal with the sociocultural contexts of all partner institutions – each with its distinctive system of education, institutional requirements, and stakeholders' conceptions of language learning, teaching, and assessment. Students involved in VE typically work collaboratively towards a common goal, but both the actual perception of the task and the level of commitment may differ depending on the students' perceptions of assessment in a given educational context and the internal assessment-related regulations in their institution. For instance, students from different educational contexts may exhibit different levels of learner autonomy and have different experiences of being assessed formatively, or may not be used to receiving criticism, no matter how constructive, from peers. It poses an additional challenge to teachers, who need to mediate these differences and collaboratively design assessment that is acceptable for all partners and meet the contextual profile at the same time.

3. Conclusions

There are five main principles of assessment – validity, reliability, authenticity, practicality, and washback (e.g. in Brown & Abeywickrama, 2010). Even though some of them are not named verbatim in the text, the discussion of the issues in assessment design presented in this chapter clearly indicate that high quality assessment in VE, similar to any other form of instruction, needs to adhere to these ground rules. The difficulty in assessing VE lies in the need to adapt FL assessment to the affordances of computer mediated communication in an intercultural and collaborative environment. In VE, both learning and assessment are learned-centred. During VE, a large portion of learning takes place outside the classroom, without teacher's supervision. This form of learning involves a high degree of learner agency and independence, which implies that teachers need to step down from a position of an evaluator, and be ready to assume a new role of a mediator and a facilitator who supports students in the process. On the other hand, these difficulties can be translated into an opportunity to introduce more formative, continuous feedback and authentic task-based assessment in VE projects, online learning, and a FL classroom at large.

References

Akiyama, Y. (2014). Review of issues and potential solutions of Japan-U.S. Telecollaboration: from the program coordinator's viewpoint. *Studies in Japanese Language Education, 11*, 3-14.

Biggs, J. (1999). *Teaching for quality learning at university*. Open University Press.

Black, P., Harrison, C., Lee, C., Marshall, B., & Wiliam D. (2004). Working inside the black box: assessment for learning in the classroom. *Phi Delta Kappan* (September), 8-21. https://doi.org/10.1177/003172170408600105

Black, P., & Wiliam, D. (1998). Inside the black box: raising standards through classroom assessment. *Phi Delta Kappan* (October), 139-148.

Brown, H. D., & Abeywickrama, P. (2010). *Language assessment: principles and classroom practice* (2nd ed.). Pearson Education Inc.

Candelier, M., Camillieri-Grima, A., Castellotti, V., de Pietro, J.-F, Lörincz, I., Meißner, F.-J., Noguerol, A., Schröder-Sura, A., & Molinié, M. (2007). *FREPA. Framework of reference for pluralistic approaches to languages and cultures*. Council of Europe and Graz: ECML. https://carap.ecml.at/

Cloke, S. (2010). The Italia-Australia intercultural project. In S. Guth & F. Helm (Eds), *Telecollaboration 2.0: language, literacies and intercultural learning in the 21st century* (pp. 375-384). Peter Lang.

Council of Europe. (2020). *Common European framework of reference for languages: learning, teaching, assessment. Companion volume*. Council of Europe Publishing. https://rm.coe.int/ common-european-framework-of-reference-for-languages-learning-teaching/16809ea0d4

Dooly, M. (2008). (Ed.). *Telecollaborative language learning. Moderating intercultural collaboration and language learning. A guidebook to moderating intercultural collaboration online*. Peter Lang.

Dooly, M. (2022). The evolution of virtual exchange and assessment practices. In A. Czura & M. Dooly (Eds), *Assessing virtual exchange in foreign language courses at tertiary level* (pp. 13-27). Research-publishing.net. https://doi.org/10.14705/rpnet.2022.59.1407

Dooly, M., & O'Dowd, R. (2012). (Eds). *Researching online foreign language interaction and exchange: theories, methods and challenges*. Peter Lang.

Dooly, M., & Vinagre, M. (2021). Research into practice: virtual exchange in language teaching and learning. *Language Teaching,* 1-15. https://doi.org/10.1017/S0261444821000069

Engelhardt, M., & Pfingsthorn, J. (2013). Self-assessment and placement tests – a worthwhile combination? *Language Learning in Higher Education, 2*(1), 75-89. https://doi.org/10.1515/cercles-2012-0005

EVOLVE Project. (2020). *The impact of virtual exchange on student learning in higher education.* http://hdl.handle.net/11370/d69d9923-8a9c-4b37-91c6-326ebbd14f17

Gallagher, G. (2017). Aligning for learning: including feedback in the constructive alignment model. *AISHE-J: The All Ireland Journal of Teaching and Learning in Higher Education, 9*(1), 3011-3019.

Green, A. (2014). *Exploring language assessment and testing: language in action.* Routledge. https://doi.org/10.4324/9781315889627

Guth, S., Helm, F., & O'Dowd, R. (2012). *University language classes collaborating online. A report on the integration of telecollaborative networks in European universities.* http://coil.suny.edu/sites/default/files/intent_report_execsummary_june2012.pdf

Hamp-Lyons, L. (2016). Purposes of assessment. In D. Tsagari & J. Banerjee (Eds), *Handbook of second language assessment* (pp. 13-28). De Gruyter/Mouton. https://doi.org/10.1515/9781614513827-004

Harlen, W., & James, M. (1997). Assessment and learning: differences and relationships between formative and summative assessment. *Assessment in Education, 4*(3), 365-380.

Hauck, M., & MacKinnon, T. (2016). A new approach to assessing online intercultural exchange: soft certifcation of participant engagement. In R. O'Dowd & T. Lewis (Eds), *Online intercultural exchange: policy, pedagogy, practice* (pp. 209-231). Routledge. https://doi.org/10.4324/9781315678931

Helm, F. (2013). A dialogic model for telecollaboration. *Bellaterra Journal of Teaching & Learning Language & Literature, 6*(2), 28-48. https://doi.org/10.5565/rev/jtl3.522

Helm, F., & van der Velden, B. (2019). *Erasmus + Virtual Exchange 2018 impact report.* Publications Office of the European Union. https://doi.org/10.2797/668291

Huerta-Macias, A. (1995). Alternative assessment: responses to commonly asked questions. *TESOL Journal, 5*(1), 8-11.

INCA Project. (2004). *Intercultural competence assessment. INCA assessor manual.* https://ec.europa.eu/migrant-integration/library-document/inca-project-intercultural-competence-assessment_en

Izmaylova, A. (2022). Assessing intercultural learning in virtual exchange. In A. Czura & M. Dooly (Eds), *Assessing virtual exchange in foreign language courses at tertiary level* (pp. 135-146). Research-publishing.net. https://doi.org/10.14705/rpnet.2022.59.1415

Koretz, D., Stecher, B., Klein, S., & McCaffrey, D. (1994). The Vermont portfolio assessment program: findings and implications. *Educational Measurement: Issues and Practice, 13*(3), 5-16. https://doi.org/10.1111/j.1745-3992.1994.tb00443.x

Kurek, M. (2015). Designing tasks for complex virtual learning environments. *Bellaterra Journal of Teaching & Learning Language & Literature, 8*(2), 13-32. https://doi.org/10.5565/rev/jtl3.633

Lee, J., & Sauro, S. (2021). Assessing language learning in virtual exchange: suggestions from the field of language assessment. *Journal of Virtual Exchange, 4*, 33-49. https://doi.org/10.21827/jve.4.36087

Lin, L., & Reinders, H. (2019). Students' and teachers' readiness for autonomy: beliefs and practices in developing autonomy in the Chinese context. *Asia Pacific Educ. Rev., 20*, 69-89. https://doi.org/10.1007/s12564-018-9564-3

Lock, C., & Munby, H. (2000). Changing assessment practices in the classroom: a study of one teacher's challenge. *Alberta Journal of Educational Research, 46*(3), 267-279.

MacKinnon, T., Ensor, S., Kleban, M., & Trégoat, C. (2020). Recognising participation in virtual exchange: open badges and the CLAVIER contribution. In F. Helm & A. Beaven (Eds), *Designing and implementing virtual exchange – a collection of case studies* (pp. 141-152). Research-publishing.net. https://doi.org/10.14705/rpnet.2020.45.1122

McMillan, J. H., & Workman, D. J. (1998). *Classroom assessment and grading practices: a review of the literature*. Metropolitan Educational Research Consortium. (ERIC Document Reproduction Service No. ED453263)

McNamara, T. (1996). *Measuring second language performance*. Addison Wesley Longman.

McNamara, T., & Roever, C. (2006). *Language testing: the social dimension*. Blackwell.

Messick, S. (1989). Validity. In R. Linn (Ed.), *Educational measurement* (pp. 13-103). American Council on Education.

Miller, M. S. (1999). Classroom assessment and university accountability. *Journal of Education for Business, 75*(2), 94-98. https://doi.org/10.1080/08832329909598997

Mont, M., & Masats, D. (2018). Tips and suggestions to implement telecollaborative projects with young learners. In M. Dooly & R. O'Dowd (Eds), *In this together: teachers' experiences with transnational, telecollaborative language learning projects*. Peter Lang.

Norris, J. (2009). Task-based teaching and testing. In M. H. Long & C. J. Doughty (Eds), *The handbook of language teaching* (pp. 578-594). Wiley-Blackwell. https://doi.org/10.1002/9781444315783.ch30

O'Dowd, R. (2010). Issues in the assessment of online interaction and exchange. In S. Guth & F. Helm (Eds), *Telecollaboration 2.0: language, literacies and intercultural learning in the 21st Century* (pp. 337-358). Peter Lang.

O'Dowd, R. (2013).Telecollaborative networks in university higher education: overcoming barriers to integration, *internet and higher education, 18*, 47-53. https://doi.org/10.1016/j.iheduc.2013.02.001

O'Dowd, R., & Ware, P. (2009). Critical issues in telecollaborative task design. *Computer Assisted Language Learning, 22*(2), 173-188. https://doi.org/10.1080/09588220902778369

Rolińska, A., & Czura, A. (2022). Assessment in the English for Academic Study Telecollaboration (EAST) project – a case study. In A. Czura & M. Dooly (Eds), *Assessing virtual exchange in foreign language courses at tertiary level* (pp. 163-175). Research-publishing.net. https://doi.org/10.14705/rpnet.2022.59.1417

Shohamy, E. (2007). Language tests as language policy tools. *Assessment in Education: Principles, Policy & Practice, 14*(1), 117-130. https://doi.org/10.1080/09695940701272948

Tierney, R. D. (2006). Changing practices: influences on classroom assessment. *Assessment in Education: Principles, Policy & Practice, 13*(3), 239-264. https://doi.org/10.1080/09695940601035387

Van den Branden, K. (2006). Introduction: task-based language teaching in a nutshell. In K. Van den Branden (Ed.), *Task-based language education: from theory to practice* (pp. 1-16). Cambridge University Press. https://doi.org/10.1017/CBO9780511667282.002

Wigglesworth, G. (2008). Task and performance based assessment. In N. H. Hornberger (Ed.), *Encyclopedia of language and education.* Springer. https://doi.org/10.1007/978-0-387-30424-3_171

3. Assessment in virtual exchange: a summary of the ASSESSnet project

Anna Czura[1] and Melinda Dooly[2]

Abstract

This chapter outlines the ASSESSnet project [ASSESSnet: Language assessment in Virtual Mobility (VM) initiatives at tertiary level – teachers' beliefs, practices and perceptions; grant number 845783; https://www.assessnet.site/home]. First, its underlying mission is explained in this introduction, before a detailed description of the compilation and analytical approach to data undertaken during the project trajectory is provided. Following the research methodology, main findings of the ASSESSnet project are summarised and conclusions drawn.

Keywords: virtual exchange, telecollaboration, assessment.

1.   Introduction

ASSESSnet was proposed to the Marie Skłodowska-Curie Individual Fellowship in 2018, and was awarded funding for 2019-2021 (extended to February of 2022). The Marie Skłodowska-Curie Actions are among Europe's most competitive and prestigious research and innovation fellowships and aim to support postdoctoral researchers' in their careers while promoting excellence in research. The funding allows fellowship recipients to carry out

---

1. Universitat Autònoma de Barcelona, Barcelona, Spain; anna.czura@uwr.edu.pl; https://orcid.org/0000-0001-5234-6618

2. Universitat Autònoma de Barcelona, Spain; melindaann.dooly@uab.cat; https://orcid.org/0000-0002-1478-4892

How to cite: Czura, A., & Dooly, M. (2022). Assessment in virtual exchange: a summary of the ASSESSnet project. In A. Czura & M. Dooly (Eds), *Assessing virtual exchange in foreign language courses at tertiary level* (pp. 47-61). Research-publishing.net. https://doi.org/10.14705/rpnet.2022.59.1409

their research activities abroad, under the supervision of more experienced researchers in their field.

The ASSESSnet project proposal was motivated by the dearth of research, teaching resources, and teacher training opportunities in the area of Virtual Exchange (VE) for language teaching and learning (Werneck Barbosa & Ferreira-Lopes, 2021). The project is centred specifically around assessment in VE in Foreign Language (FL) courses, looking particularly at tertiary level across different educational contexts, with the goal of contributing to this gap in educational research.

The general goal of the ASSESSnet project is to support FL practitioners in the process of assessing student learning in VEs, particularly in terms of selecting appropriate assessment content, criteria, and tools. In order to complete these aims, the project focused on these central objectives:

- investigating teachers' beliefs about the assessment objectives, practices, and content in VE in order to identify teachers' rationale behind the choice of classroom assessment method and content;

- exploring the planning of the assessment process in VE. This research objective aimed at identifying the stakeholders involved in the planning of the assessment process and grading policy (i.e. the role of the teacher, the home, and partner institutions and learners);

- investigating the implementation of assessment in VE. Here, the objective was to investigate the share of responsibility between the involved stakeholders, timeline of gathering evidence, approaches to providing feedback, and the documentation of assessment;

- analysing the form of assessment in VM projects at tertiary level. Within this objective we addressed the types of assessment measures (both formal and informal) applied by teachers to verify learning outcomes in

VE projects. In particular, the use of specific assessment tools (e.g. tests, portfolios, projects, peer assessment, etc.) was explored;

- identifying the content of assessment in VE. This objective focused on establishing the construct of assessment and how its content was aligned with course objectives and activities.

The mixed approach of both quantitative and qualitative data collection and analysis was chosen as the best means to fully explore the values, perspectives, experiences, and worldviews of the VE practitioners around the world (see research methodology below for a detailed description). This allowed for a rich, wider scale of examples of innovative, effective methods regarding assessment practices, materials, and tools specifically aimed at language learning in VE at university. The characteristics of the respondents is noteworthy given that the majority hold more than a decade of experience in language teaching, which speaks of the quality of the perspectives collected. There is also a significant representation of languages taught as well as contexts in which the VE has been carried out (see section below), which accentuates the diversity of views and experiences presented and discussed. The heterogeneity of contexts also highlights the relevance of the institutional parameters contingent to the VEs when it comes to assessment procedures, as is discussed in this book.

There are some result outcomes that can be highlighted, beginning with the emphasis that many of the respondents place on the facet of assessment as key support for student learning and as a means of providing students informative feedback on both the process and the product of learning. This is of specific relevance for instances of VE that take place outside of 'regular' class timetables and in many cases, without teacher/instructor presence. This places additional weight on learner autonomy and its role in the overall assessment of VE. Relative to this, the question of whether the VE is a compulsory or voluntary part of the overall institutional parameter of the course also comes into account when designing assessment for VE.

Inevitably, the very nature of compiling, synthesising, and publishing the results may seem to imply straight-cut procedures that belie the complexity of carrying out evaluation in this type of exchanges. In this chapter we do not endeavour to deny these inherent difficulties; on the contrary, the challenges of assessment in VE are acknowledged and even embraced as part and parcel of the results presented herein.

2. Research methodology

The data was principally collected by means of an online questionnaire and interviews. The former consisted of Likert-type, rating scales, and open-ended questions. This tool, available in four languages (English, Spanish, Catalan, and Polish), was designed to explore teacher beliefs as regards assessment objectives, tools, and content. The in-depth oral expert interviews centred on the teachers' attitudes to assessment and grading, as well as their assessment practices, instruments, and strategies in courses involving elements of VE. The interview data was transcribed and content analysed. The combination of these two instruments gave us a more thorough understanding of the assessment procedures used in different contexts. These data were supplemented with the analysis of assessment-related resources and documents (e.g. syllabi, assessment rubrics, descriptions of assessment tools) provided by some research participants.

In order to collect the relevant data, we contacted many associations of tertiary level education and university FL centres; we sent individual invitations to over 200 teachers involved in VE. Despite the difficult time of the Covid-19 pandemic, which necessitated a sudden shift from in-class to online teaching, 63 teachers volunteered to complete the questionnaire and 33 took part in the interview. Due to the international nature of VE projects, the foreign/second language teachers who took part in the study teach in a wide range of higher education institutions (HEIs) in Europe and beyond (e.g. United States, Mexico, Brazil, Japan, Oman). As many as 85% of the participants have been teaching a foreign/second language for over ten years (with 51%

teaching more than 20 years), which suggests that the research group consisted of practitioners with extensive teaching experience. English, indicated by 46 respondents, proved to be the most widely taught language. It was followed by Spanish (17 teachers), German (7), French (4), Chinese and Italian (3), and Japanese and Portuguese (2). Arabic, Catalan, Polish, Russian, and Swedish were taught by individual teachers.

3. Summary of research findings

The ASSESSnet study revealed that the approaches to assessment are highly diversified across educational contexts and tend to differ from institution to institution, but also from teacher to teacher within one HEI. It reflects the diversity of VE projects carried out around the globe and reported in the subject literature. Yet, some common observations can be made as regards teachers' approaches to assessment, the use of particular assessment tools, but also problems practitioners struggle with assessing student learning in VE. This section summarises the main project findings in terms of the role of the institution and teachers in assessment, the latter's beliefs about assessment objectives, practices, and tools, as well as how these beliefs are translated into classroom instruction.

3.1. Same or different?

On the inter-institutional level, parallel approaches to assessment adopted by all VE partners facilitate, but are not essential to the success of the assessment process. Minor differences deriving from, for instance, the institutional requirements or assessment standards, or different course objectives typically do not hinder student involvement and task completion, as long as the assessment procedures in the respective institutions share common points that all students can easily relate to. To this end, students in all institutions need to be appointed clearly defined roles, be involved in the same or parallel tasks, and work towards precisely stated objectives. This can be achieved when all teachers involved in VE discuss and agree on assessment formats, criteria, and tools well in advance, and continue cooperating closely to ensure consistency throughout the project. Institutional recognition of students' work in the form of grades or credit points proves to be a key factor that fosters more sustained cooperation among students and, thus, increases the likelihood of task completion. Many of these findings are anthologised in this book. For instance, the examples of projects in which students, despite different course objectives and assessment regulations in partner institutions, collaborated successfully within clearly defined roles can be found in chapters by Cavalari and Aranha (2022, this volume), Dolcini and Matthias Phelps (2022, this volume) and Vuylsteke (2022, this volume).

On the other hand, as described in chapter eleven (Rolińska & Czura, 2022, this volume) a significant imbalance in approaches to assessment between the partners may result in students' dissatisfaction, decreased commitment, and even withdrawal from the project. This happens particularly when in one partner institution VE learning objectives are integrated into the course and assessment, whereas the students in the other institution contribute on a voluntary basis and/or do not see any tangible gains from such a time investment. To overcome this imbalance, in courses in which VE constitutes a voluntary component of the course, some research participants try to integrate students' contribution in such projects into a formal assessment procedure. For instance, in appreciation of students' time and effort invested in VE, they may be exempted from selected regular course assignments as long as they hand in specific reflective tasks or outputs of the collaborative efforts in the VE project. This way, instead of submitting a writing task assigned in the course, the VE participants prepare a text that reflects their contribution to the virtual and collaborative practice. In other contexts, the participants sometimes received a certificate or a virtual badge in recognition of knowledge and skills they have acquired in the course of VE. Such certificates, however, do not always prove sufficient to motivate students to complete the course.

3.2. The purpose of assessment in VE

This brings us to the definition of what constitutes assessment in VE. The ASSESSnet project aimed to explore teachers' beliefs about the assessment objectives, practices, and content in VE. In respect to the first element, the results suggest that the teachers are principally oriented towards formative objectives of assessment. In this light, assessment is viewed as a continuous process targeted at improving different facets of student learning and as a tool that offers students informative feedback on both the process and the product of learning. As most of the students' work takes place outside of the classroom, assessment is also perceived as an important source of information used by teachers to address students' needs, solve problems, improve the running of the current project, and facilitate instructional planning.

Most of the participants believe that assessment is an essential element of VE. Firstly, assessment is seen as an important motivator that pushes students to engage in the course and complete the assigned tasks, such as a presentation, a poster, or a website. Secondly, formative and continuous assessment, which, according to the research participants, lies at the heart of assessment in VE, enables teachers to guide or coach their students in a secure, guided environment. Reflective (self-) assessment tasks encourage students to pay a closer attention to the quality of their collaborative work, problem solving skills, and the meaning of the intercultural experience. This underscores the importance of incorporating VE into a regular study programme on the institutional level – being granted a grade and/or credit points for their time and work investment, students are more likely to not only commit to the assigned tasks, but also engage in activities on a deeper level and benefit from the learning gains afforded by these projects.

3.3. Assessment practices

As regards the assessment practices, rather than using one assessment tool only, the teachers tend to devise assessment procedures that consist of an array of different tools, which allows for collecting different types of student output and assessing students on multiple occasions throughout the project. Applying diverse assessment tools within one project enables the teachers to use assessment information both for summative, which is sometimes required by the institution, and formative purposes. Traditional tests, used initially by a few research participants, have proven ill-suited for the dynamics and complexity of student work in VE settings. Unlike O'Dowd's (2010) findings, assessing students on the basis of participation and the frequency of submissions only, rather than their quality, is sporadic, and when it does occur, the pass/fail grading option is usually supplemented with more detailed feedback.

Except for e-tandem projects, i.e. bilingual exchange projects during which students usually discuss specific topics with their language learning partners, the pedagogical design of VE projects is predominantly task-based – students are typically asked to carry out a concrete task or a series of tasks that produce clear outcomes, e.g. a project, presentation, website, poster, or report. Such task-based assessment is particularly noticeable in, but not exclusive to, Foreign Language for Specific Purposes (FLSP) courses, where task-based and content-based assessment aims to engage students in Computer-Mediated Communication (CMC) on topics related to their field of study, and thus promotes authenticity and FL use in potential professional communicative contexts (cf. Czura, 2021). These communicative tasks constitute the basis of both formative and summative assessment. While working towards the collaborative output, students are usually asked to reflect on and document their experience, e.g. in the form of a portfolio or a learning diary, and receive ongoing teacher and/or peer feedback on the progress they make towards goal accomplishment. Depending on the VE project, the final outcome is handed in to the teacher or presented in front of the class and subject to peer assessment. Both teacher and peer assessment is typically based on a set of clearly defined criteria the students are familiar with. Teachers' approaches to making the summative decisions vary; however, in most cases the final grade or a mark is awarded on the basis of the cumulative evaluation of the final task, the subtasks (if applicable) as well as students' commitment to collaborative work and reflective practice. As can be seen, the implementation of formative and summative assessment tools in task-based projects allows for assessing both the process of working on a task and the final product.

Regardless of the VE type, students' assignments essentially involve some degree of collaboration with VE partners – the cooperation may consist in planning and completing a task together or providing one another with constructive peer feedback. For some teachers peer feedback and peer assessment lie at the heart of assessment in VE as they create an opportunity for students to exchange their expertise in content-related and/or linguistic aspects and work towards a common goal. To further foster a process-approach to task completion, in some courses students are offered one or several rounds of feedback before the final outcome is due. Since some students are not used to giving and receiving feedback from peers, preparatory courses or training resources that would guide students on how to offer constructive criticism in a reciprocal way have proven useful in many contexts.

The ASSESSnet research participants underline the importance of engaging students in the practice of guided self-reflection throughout the VE experience to help them gain a better awareness of autonomous learning, as well as linguistic and intercultural growth. Additionally, since most of student learning takes place outside the classroom in collaborative dyads or groups, students' reflections give teachers valuable insight into the quality and effectiveness of collaborative practice. Students' reflections are typically documented in a portfolio/e-portfolio or a learning diary and may, depending on the VE objectives, focus on the quality of collaborative activities, language learning incidents, content-based learning, or the use of learning and communication strategies (cf. Cavalari & Aranha, 2022, this volume). Such portfolio or diary entries are often guided through specific prompts provided by the teacher (examples available in Dolcini & Matthias Phelps, 2022, this volume). Reflective practice may be also fostered through mediation sessions, i.e. fairly regular one-to-one or group meetings, which create a platform for exchanging learning experiences and solving ongoing problems (e.g. Elstermann, 2022, this volume). Such sessions may be based on students' portfolio and diary entries or be organised as stand-alone meetings, during which students share and re-examine their experience *ad hoc* or on the basis of a script that, if the teacher chooses, concentrates on a selected aspect of VE experience, such as communication strategies, national stereotypes, and digital literacies.

Among the less frequently used assessment tools are recordings of students' online interactions. Teachers admit that they do not typically listen to all the recordings, but rather use them as a back-up option to be explored in cases of potential problems or miscommunications between students. In one project, to facilitate the final task completion, all collaborating students are encouraged to use the recorded interaction to prepare their group reports in greater detail. Additionally, students are sometimes asked to submit for assessment a selected recording of their online interaction that matches specific criteria indicated earlier by the teacher.

3.4. Content of assessment

Concerning the content, according to the questionnaire results, intercultural competence, online communication, and collaboration constitute main assessment criteria in VE. These three elements lie at the heart of formative assessment, which gives teachers an insight of what is happening during online interactions. The sampling of practices in our study show that except for a few cases when teachers evaluate recordings of synchronous interactions, online communication is not usually attended to directly. Additionally, unless for research purposes, teachers do not aim to measure the longitudinal development of intercultural or linguistic competences before and after the VE project. This implies that teachers prefer to act as facilitators of learning these competences rather than judges. Even though the questionnaire suggests that accuracy is seen as moderately important, many interviewees admit that they take different measures to attend to the quality of language the students produce. For instance, students' reports, selected portfolio entries, or presentations outlining VE project outcomes are often assessed on the basis of rubrics that, depending on the task and project objectives, consist of such criteria as linguistic accuracy, the range of vocabulary and grammatical structures, coherence, organisation of the text, the required content, etc. The last element is often linked with evaluating students' selected academic skills as in order to complete an assignment in task-based assessment students often need to search for, select, and synthesise information from various sources. It is particularly noticeable in FLSP courses, in which teachers additionally pay attention to the subject-specific content (business, tourism, technology, etc.)

3.5. Recurring challenges

Nevertheless, teachers voice a number of concerns as regards assessment in VE courses. First of all, there are limited training opportunities, textbooks, and teaching resources that aim specifically at assessment-related teaching competences in VE. And indeed, the questionnaire indicates that the level of training in assessment proves to be lower in comparison with other aspects of running a VE. They admit that due to the shortage of resources and training opportunities, their approaches to assessment have evolved through trial and error over the years, and some participants still struggle to find assessment tools that would target competencies triggered by intercultural and collaborative online exchanges. Ready-made resources containing clear assessment guidelines and VE scenarios, e.g. developed by the ICCAGE project (2017), used by a few participants, have proven useful, especially to teachers who are new to designing and running VE projects.

When asked about the most pressing training needs, the majority of participants point out that easier access to examples and case studies depicting assessment approaches in different contexts would greatly support their instructional planning. Additionally, the assessment of intercultural aspects and collaboration skills – in terms of defining the construct and selecting appropriate elicitation tools – is perceived as challenging. In the context of FLSP learning, some teachers who do not have subject-specific education and experience found the assessment of subject-related content problematic.

Given its predominantly formative nature, assessment in VE involves a significant time and workload on the part of the teachers and students. This should be recognised by HEI managerial staff in charge of calculating time commitment of teachers running such courses and course credits in the case of students. The ASSESSnet study indicates that in the contexts where teachers' workload and effort were appreciated on the institutional level, the assessment procedures these teachers applied tended to be more elaborate in terms of tools, criteria used, and feedback provision.

4. Conclusions

There are many emergent themes that can be found in the ASSESSnet findings, however, for sake of brevity we will foreground points which will be useful for VE practitioners. In particular, we look at the need for recognition, coordination, and mutual respect regarding how each partner/institution assesses their pupils in the VE; authenticity in VE language and intercultural assessment and perhaps most importantly, the need for training in assessment procedures in VE.

VE consists of collaboration – between students, teachers, and even institutions – in order for the outcomes to be beneficial for learning. This includes the design, the implementation, and the assessment. Therefore all partner institutions should be considered as important stakeholders that affect the shape and the perceived significance of the assessment process. This does not mean that the partners must have identical assessment procedures since the course and institutional parameters, language levels and learning goals may differ for the partners involved. However, agreement on relevance of assessment and an understanding of how assessment will be dealt with by each partner is paramount. Tangential to this, the results indicate that regardless of the goals and content of the VE, some degree of collaboration with VE partners must occur; otherwise this very nature of the VE is set to fail (Dooly & Vinagre, 2021). This implies that collaboration should be included in assessment from all partner teachers, usually in the form of constructive peer feedback, given that many of the VE activities take part outside of the classroom and without the teachers being present.

The nature of VE also comes into play regarding the authenticity of language assessment in these exchanges. As Czura (2021) points out, VE is typically implemented with the aim to engage students in 'real' communication (CMC) on topics related to their field of study, often through the use of a target FL. This engagement is promoted outside the classroom and therefore goes beyond more controlled, target language use to include contexts where the learners must use the language to communicate ideas, opinions, to argue their points, and to work together to achieve common goals. This authenticity extends to the assessment procedures in VE in which task outcomes are "authentically representative of tasks in the target situation" (Douglas, 2000, p. 19). Additionally, since VE is often about interactions that involve heterogeneity regarding participants' socio-geographical backgrounds, assessment typically aims to include these aspects in the criteria, reflecting intercultural gains and the ability to interact competently in variegated communicative situations and with diverse groups.

The results of the study also indicate that teachers' beliefs about assessment objectives in VE are closely correlated to their assessment practices. In most cases, the experienced teachers indicated that they perceive assessment as being highly formative and therefore their assessment practices, in turn, included the means for continuous collection of evidence that can indicate evolution and learning gains such as rubrics, self and peer assessment, portfolios, diaries, etc. Formative assessment tools were also seen as an important element of promoting learner autonomy, and offering students guidance on language learning, effective collaborative engagement, and dealing with intercultural communication. Such a scaffolded support to fostering learner autonomy is of particular importance in contexts in which most of the learning takes place outside the classroom and without teacher's direct supervision (Czura & Baran-Lucarz, 2021).

Many of the respondents lamented their own lack of training opportunities when first starting out with VE and zeroed in on the need for language teachers' access to examples and training opportunities, not only for designing and implementing VE but also more specifically for dealing with the complexity of assessing language learning that occurs in relatively short timespans (usually a semester or less) and in technological environments that may, at times, impede the communication and which are singular in their reliance on learner autonomy. This spotlights the need for examples and case studies (such as produced by this project) as well as the importance of networks of practitioners that facilitate the exchange of experiences and teaching and assessing resources, in particular for novice VE teachers.

It is necessary to point out the inherent limitations of these findings. The number of respondents for qualitative data is significant (63 completed questionnaires;

33 interviews) and quite heterogeneous, ensuring variegated perspectives and practices. However, it is recognised that these conclusions were formulated on the basis of responses provided by participants who kindly responded to our invitation and agreed to participate on voluntary basis in this study. This implies a prior engagement and interest in the theme and therefore cannot be treated as a fully representative picture of assessment approaches adopted in all settings. Nevertheless, the results of the study offer valuable insight into both the institutional and pedagogical aspects of assessing student learning in such complex environments as VE projects.

This study lays the foundation for fruitful research in the near future. Given the growing importance of VE in higher education, there will be ample opportunities – and need for – further exploration into the solid assessment procedures in VE in FL courses, not only at tertiary level, but also across all ages and levels; especially as this educational practice becomes more extensively applied around the world. Attention needs to be given to longitudinal studies that trace in-class cohorts of established VE partnerships to better detect gains outside of the immediate learning context. Such studies will also lay the foundations for a detailed analysis of constructive alignment between the objectives, tasks, and assessment. There are also few studies on VE for beginners (both as research on design and implementation as well as assessment). This may be due to lack of confidence or fear of the complexity of setting up VEs for beginner learners.

References

Cavalari, S., & Aranha, S. (2022). Learners' diaries as a tool for teachers' assessment in teletandem. In A. Czura & M. Dooly (Eds), *Assessing virtual exchange in foreign language courses at tertiary level* (pp. 65-78). Research-publishing.net. https://doi.org/10.14705/rpnet.2022.59.1410

Czura, A. (2021). Virtual exchange in foreign language for specific purposes courses: assessment strategies and tools. *Multilingual academic and professional communication in a networked world. Proceedings of AELFE-TAPP 2021.* http://hdl.handle.net/2117/348620

Czura A., & Baran-Lucarz, M. (2021). "A stressful unknown" or "an oasis"?: undergraduate students' perceptions of assessment in an in-class and online English phonetics course. *Íkala, 26*(3), 623-641. https://doi.org/10.17533/udea.ikala.v26n3a09

Dolcini, G., & Matthias Phelps, G. (2022). Is (inter)cultural competence accessible? Assessing for fluency. In A. Czura & M. Dooly (Eds), *Assessing virtual exchange in foreign language courses at tertiary level* (pp. 123-134). Research-publishing.net. https://doi.org/10.14705/rpnet.2022.59.1414

Dooly, M., & Vinagre, M. (2021). Research into practice: virtual exchange in language teaching and learning. *Language Teaching*, 1-15. https://doi.org/10.1017/S0261444821000069

Douglas, D. (2000). *Assessing languages for specific purposes*. Cambridge University Press. https://doi.org/10.1017/CBO9780511732911

Elstermann, A.-K. (2022). Peer group mediation sessions as an assessment tool in teletandem. In A. Czura & M. Dooly (Eds), *Assessing virtual exchange in foreign language courses at tertiary level* (pp. 79-91). Research-publishing.net. https://doi.org/10.14705/rpnet.2022.59.1411

ICCAGE project. (2017). *Intercultural communicative competence: open educational resources*. https://iccageproject.wixsite.com/presentation/innovative-icc-educational-materials

O'Dowd, R. (2010). Issues in the assessment of online interaction and exchange. In S. Guth & F. Helm (Eds), *Telecollaboration 2.0: language, literacies and intercultural learning in the 21st century* (pp. 337-358). Peter Lang.

Rolińska, A., & Czura, A. (2022). Assessment in the English for Academic Study Telecollaboration (EAST) project – a case study. In A. Czura & M. Dooly (Eds), *Assessing virtual exchange in foreign language courses at tertiary level* (pp. 163-175). Research-publishing.net. https://doi.org/10.14705/rpnet.2022.59.1417

Vuylsteke, J.-F. (2022). Business communication skills through virtual exchange – a case study. In A. Czura & M. Dooly (Eds), *Assessing virtual exchange in foreign language courses at tertiary level* (pp. 147-162). Research-publishing.net. https://doi.org/10.14705/rpnet.2022.59.1416

Werneck Barbosa, M., & Ferreira-Lopes, L. (2021 early view). Emerging trends in telecollaboration and virtual exchange: a bibliometric study. *Educational Review*. https://doi.org/10.1080/00131911.2021.1907314

Part 2.
Assessment tools in virtual exchange

4. Learners' diaries as a tool for teachers' assessment in teletandem

Suzi Marques Spatti Cavalari[1] and Solange Aranha[2]

Abstract

The purpose of this chapter is to present the assessment practice carried out by means of learning diaries within institutionally integrated teletandem, a bilingual model of Virtual Exchange (VE) embedded into foreign language courses at São Paulo State University (UNESP), in Brazil. Teachers read learners' diaries on a weekly basis and provide one-to-one feedback related to (1) telecollaborative learning processes, (2) difficulties and affective factors, and (3) linguistic aspects. This asynchronous form of assessment in the form of teachers' feedback on learners' diaries not only guides each individual learner's autonomous learning, but also allows teachers to select relevant information to be used in synchronous group discussions and teaching in face-to-face lessons.

Keywords: learning diaries, formative assessment, teletandem.

1. Introduction

Classroom assessment practices are generally defined and described in relation to the purposes they have: summative assessment is carried out with the purpose of accountability (i.e. to grade and classify students' work), usually at the end of a period of instruction; formative assessment, on the other hand, is carried out

---

1. São Paulo State University, São Paulo, Brazil; suzi.cavalari@unesp.br; https://orcid.org/0000-0001-7748-8516

2. São Paulo State University, São Paulo, Brazil; solange.aranha@unesp.br; https://orcid.org/0000-0002-8092-1875

How to cite: Cavalari, S. M. S., & Aranha, S. (2022). Learners' diaries as a tool for teachers' assessment in teletandem. In A. Czura & M. Dooly (Eds), *Assessing virtual exchange in foreign language courses at tertiary level* (pp. 65-78). Research-publishing.net. https://doi.org/10.14705/rpnet.2022.59.1410

concurrently with instruction and serves the purpose of guiding teaching and learning (Black & Wiliam, 1998). They are both legitimate forms of evaluation in educational settings and are likely to be used in an integrated way (Black & Wiliam, 2009), i.e. tests designed with a summative purpose may be utilized also to inform teaching and learning.

VE is "an embedded, dialogic process that supports geographically distanced collaborative work through social interaction, involving a/synchronous communication technology so that participants co-produce mutual objective(s) and share knowledge-building" (Sadler & Dooly, 2016, p. 2). As a classroom integrated project, VE is commonly assessed by means of different tools, depending on the goals of the exchange. The concept of classroom assessment, according to Black and Wiliam (1998), encompasses activities carried out both by teachers and students, which can be used as feedback to provide information to modify the teaching-learning process in which they are engaged. This definition seems particularly relevant for VE contexts due to three aspects. Firstly, it proposes that assessment can be carried out through any activity participants are engaged in. Because telecollaboration involves different pedagogical tasks by means of which students should learn and co-construct knowledge, any of these tasks could be used as an assessment tool. Also, the concept includes both teachers and students as agents of assessment. In VE projects, due to its inherently collaborative nature, it seems coherent that all the agents (teachers, students, and students' VE partners) should be involved in assessment practice that can guide teaching-learning activities. Finally, it suggests that classroom evaluative practice should be oriented by a formative perspective, and it emphasizes the critical role feedback plays in assessment. Feedback is central because it fosters what Black and Wiliam (2009) call formative interaction: synchronous or asynchronous "'moments of contingency' in instruction[3] for the purpose of the regulation of learning processes" (p. 12). The authors explain that moments of contingency are characterized by (1) real-time adjustments teachers make during one-to-one instruction or whole class discussion, (2) feedback teachers provide through

---

3. The authors consider that instruction involves both teaching and learning processes.

grading practices (and through evidence derived from homework), or (3) feedback students offer at the end of a lesson to plan a subsequent lesson, for example (Black & Wiliam, 2009, pp. 10, 11).

In VE projects, besides getting feedback from their teachers, students have opportunities to give and receive feedback in a reciprocal way by means of different tools while interacting with peers and carrying out the various tasks proposed. Based on these tenets, we aim at presenting the assessment practice carried out in institutionally integrated teletandem, a bilingual model of VE based on the tandem principles. We focus on the formative purpose of assessment by describing teachers' feedback on learners' learning diaries. According to Moon (2010), reflective/learning diaries or journals are terms that can be used to refer to the engagement of learners in registering "ongoing issues over time" with the purpose or "intention to learn from either the process of doing it or from the results of it" (p. 3). In this chapter, the terms 'learning diary' and 'reflexive diary' are used interchangeably. From within the theoretical framework briefly presented, the use of diaries involves both the learner's and the teacher's perspectives in the assessment practice. As learners write their diaries, they are expected to reflect upon and monitor their learning, which implies a selection of the information they consider relevant. As teachers read their learners' diaries and provide feedback, they can select the information that they consider pertinent to guide teaching and learning. We intend to present teachers' feedback, focusing on the kind of information that is selected and how this seems to create moments of formative interaction to guide the teaching-learning process.

2. Overview of the teletandem project

Teletandem (Telles & Vassallo, 2006) is a bilingual VE project in which speakers of different languages (who live in different countries) are paired up in order to learn each other's language and culture by means of videoconferencing tools. It was introduced at UNESP in 2006, and more recently has been adopted in other institutions (cf. Aranha & Cavalari, 2021

– www.teletandembrasil.org). Throughout the years, the practice has been adjusted to fit the needs of the different cohorts and the various contexts in which the practice is implemented. Until 2020, nearly 8,000 university students have participated in the project at three of the university's *campi*: Assis, São José do Rio Preto, and Araraquara. The concept and the approach of this VE is based on the tandem principles (Brammerts, 1996; Telles, 2006) of reciprocity (each participant should collaborate with his/her partner's learning), separation of languages (each language must have a separate moment of practice), and autonomy (each participant should be responsible for his/her own learning).

Teletandem can be implemented in diverse modalities (institutionally non-integrated, semi-integrated, and integrated) that depend on how institutionally and pedagogically integrated the practice is on both sides of the partnership. We focus on the organizational proposal of institutionally integrated teletandem (iiTTD), as described by Aranha and Cavalari (2014) and Cavalari and Aranha (2016). In this modality, at São José do Rio Preto, dyads of English and Portuguese speakers meet once a week, during eight weeks. Teletandem tasks are connected to the English course syllabi in 'Language Teacher Education' and 'Translations Studies' undergraduate programs. The tasks are related to the overall objectives of the VE (learning a foreign language and culture) and of the EFL (English as a Foreign Language) courses, and consist in developing linguistic intercultural skills and improving the overall communicative competence.

The learning design is organized into two macro tasks (Aranha & Leone, 2017), the Teletandem Oral Sessions (TOSs) and the Teletandem Mediation Sessions, which are organized in various micro tasks. The TOSs are the conversations between pairs of university students via a videoconferencing tool. Mediation sessions are meetings in which the teacher/mediator and the group of students discuss problems encountered during TOSs, achievements related to different competences, evaluation of the learning process, and other issues raised by the participation in the project. The micro tasks are carried out by the students with the purpose of helping them prepare for the participation in the macro tasks. These include:

- answering questionnaires – a pre-project questionnaire (to self-evaluate proficiency level and set learning goals) and a post-project questionnaire (to assess the teletandem experience and the extent to which learning goals have been met);

- attending a tutorial (orientation meeting) that gives learners an overview of the project;

- writing reflexive diaries after each TOS;

- producing a text, video, or audio (depending on the course teletandem is integrated in) in the foreign language one is learning (and sharing it with the teletandem partner); and

- offering feedback to the oral or written production in one's native language.

Each of the micro tasks may be used as an assessment instrument, either with a formative or a summative purpose, in line with the specificities of the learning scenario in which teletandem is integrated. In general, teachers tend to grade students' participation by means of reflexive diaries, and their achievements by means of the (final version of the) collaborative outcome, i.e. text, video, or audio files. As far as the authors of this chapter are concerned, no rubrics have been created so far for either of these assessment instruments.

In this chapter, we address specifically the formative assessment practice carried out by teachers as they provide feedback on learning diaries. We present examples of diaries written by Brazilians participating in exchanges with students from the UK and from the USA, between 2016 and 2020. According to Cavalari and Aranha (2016), the learning diary is an instrument "to stimulate ongoing reflection about the learning process" (p. 332). Participants are expected to reflect upon their teletandem experience, ponder over any difficulties they might be facing (and possible solutions), and evaluate their progress toward the learning goals they have set when they answered the initial questionnaire. In the initial phase of the project, during the tutorial, the teacher presents questions to guide learners as they write their diaries[4].

> "After each teletandem oral session, it is essential that you write a learning diary. Writing the diaries aims at helping you reflect upon what happens during the sessions and how you can benefit from the experience. When you write your diary, try to reflect on:
>
> - Which topics were discussed during that specific session? What did you learn?
>
> - Go back to the learning goals you set when you answered the initial questionnaire. Explain how your participation in the project has been helping you achieve them. If you conclude that you might be on the wrong track, think about ways to make adjustments.
>
> - Make comments about (1) moments in which there was any conflict, or you faced any difficulty; (2) the causes for that; and (3) how (or if) the problem was solved.
>
> - Has your partner been supporting your learning process? How? Did you negotiate these issues during the session?"

Learners can decide if they want to write their diaries in English or in Portuguese, and they should write one diary entry per week on *Google Docs®* after each teletandem oral session. These entries are stored in a personal folder on *Google Drive®* that is shared with the teacher. The diaries are given weekly feedback by the teacher who can select recurrent and/or relevant issues to be discussed in the mediation sessions held during face-to-face language lessons (Cavalari & Aranha, 2019).

---

4. These guidelines were translated by the authors. The original text can be found on the website: https://teletandemriopreto.wixsite.com/ibilce/como-produzir-o-diario

3. Assessment by means of learners' diaries

From the formative perspective, feedback is considered an essential element of assessment since it may foster regulation of the teaching-learning process. To describe formative assessment practice by means of learning diaries, we focus on the feedback provided by different teachers who read teletandem participants' diaries on a weekly basis. We present what teachers focused on, i.e. the content of the feedback, and how teachers provide feedback, i.e. the strategies they use. We also discuss how offering one-to-one feedback seems to enable teachers to collect information that may feed group discussions in face-to-face lessons (mediation sessions) and guide the teaching-learning process in the VE.

3.1. Feedback related to learning aspects in iiTTD

The most common content of teachers' feedback is related to different aspects of learning in teletandem. When learners vaguely (or do not) mention their learning, teachers try to encourage them to reflect upon it.

Figure 1. 2016_UK_diary02

> *Try to share things you have been learning.*
> *Where is your first diary? You missed the first interaction?*

The feedback is inserted in a different color at the end of the diary entry. The teacher nudges the participant to reflect on his learning process and achievements in the following entries and asks about the accomplishment of another task – the TOS. A missing diary entry may result from a student's absence from the oral session. This strategy may foster autonomous learning in teletandem, and, at the same time, allows the teacher to be updated about the accomplishment of the VE tasks.

Teachers' feedback also focuses on teletandem guiding principles. Figure 2 emphasizes the role that teletandem principles play in this learning setting and draws students' attention to the collaborative (reciprocal) aspect that ensures the mutual benefits that the practice should offer. This type of feedback reinforces the guidelines teachers give students in the tutorial (and in mediation sessions). This reinforcement may serve the purpose of positive feedback, by telling students what seems to be going right.

Figure 2. 2020_USA_ diary03[5]

help him with a reliable material and ask him to discuss said topics with me during the session. This mechanism of using our Portuguese speaking time with topics that matter to his learning and using the English speaking time with topics that help mine is really working out for both of us.	yay!! that means you guys really understand how to make the best out of this experience. I am so glad for the both of you.

Teachers also address intercultural aspects in teletandem learning. In Figure 3, the student mentions holidays and festivities in both countries.

Figure 3. 2015_USA_diary05[6]

The last interaction was the most productive of all. It was the only one that began in time, so there was enough time for my partner to revise my text, making some few changes, and for us to talk about the subject of my seminar, which helped me a lot. Then we switched to Portuguese and talked about festivities like Halloween and Christmas, comparing how they work in each country, and also some festivities that don't exist in the other's country. In this	It is always interesting what cultures might have in common and how they may be different from each other. What have you discovered during this conversation?

The teacher highlights the relevance of 'comparing and contrasting' cultural elements that arise during the oral interactions. As several studies[7] on telecollaborative learning have showed, looking for similarities and differences in how cultural issues are perceived in different countries is essential to foster the development of intercultural competence. It is relevant to consider that this feedback includes a question that the student may answer if he/she wishes. Experience has shown that students tend to answer this type of question in the following diary entry, triggering asynchronous moments of contingency.

---

5. A more readable version of this figure can be viewed online in supplementary materials.

6. A more readable version of this figure can be viewed online in supplementary materials.

7. c.f. Levet (2015) and other studies on the Cultura Project: http://cultura.mit.edu/publications

3.2. Feedback related to students' difficulties and emotions

Teachers' feedback is also focused on students' struggles and feelings. Figure 4 shows that the Brazilian learner is facing interpersonal difficulties, and he seems to be frustrated by the fact that his partner is shy and does not collaborate as expected.

Figure 4. 2020_USA_diary04[8]

> I feel that I could have learned more info if my partner wasn't so shy. He doesn't speak a lot and I have to force conversation almost all the time. what really doesn't make I feel the reciprocity. At the end of the session, I asked him to PLEASE send me an email if he ever find some subject that we wants to talk about, but he didn't yet. Hope the next session be better than this one.
>
> that can be frustrating, _____, however, remember that part of the information you are going to present in the seminar must come from searching sources on the internet (for example, statistics, essays and articles, etc). Then, you could use what you have found to ask him more questions - and his view on the subject

The teacher tries to be sympathetic about the American partner's nonreciprocal attitude. At the same time, she suggests that the Brazilian student uses the collaborative task proposed for this learning scenario (the collaborative creation of a PowerPoint presentation on a cultural topic) as support for the oral interaction. Just like in Figure 1, this type of feedback sheds light on the connections among the various tasks that teletandem participants are expected to carry out as a form of support for their learning. In this sense, formative assessment by means of teacher's feedback on learning diaries seems to encourage the integration of face-to-face and telecollaborative practice, as proposed by Cavalari and Aranha (2016).

Figure 5 refers to the challenges the Brazilian student faces to explain relative clauses (in Portuguese) to her American partner. Even though it is an EFL course, the teacher's feedback entails a connection between teletandem practice and face-to-face EFL lessons within a teacher education program.

---

8. A more readable version of this figure can be viewed online in supplementary materials.

Chapter 4

Figure 5. 2016_UK_diary03[9]

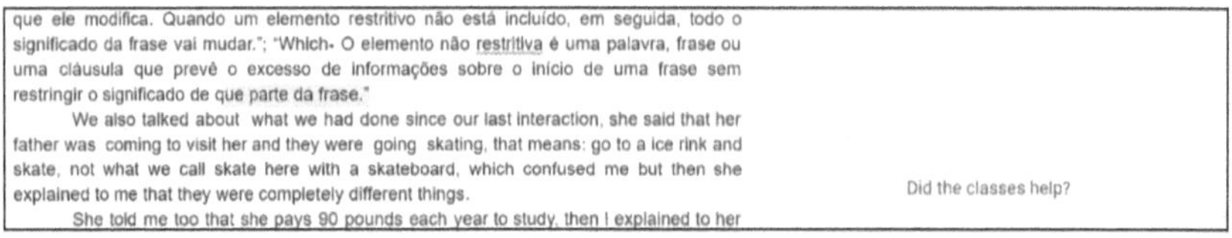

> que ele modifica. Quando um elemento restritivo não está incluido, em seguida, todo o significado da frase vai mudar."; "Which- O elemento não restritiva é uma palavra, frase ou uma cláusula que prevê o excesso de informações sobre o início de uma frase sem restringir o significado de que parte da frase."
>   We also talked about what we had done since our last interaction, she said that her father was coming to visit her and they were going skating, that means: go to a ice rink and skate, not what we call skate here with a skateboard, which confused me but then she explained to me that they were completely different things.   *Did the classes help?*
>   She told me too that she pays 90 pounds each year to study, then I explained to her

It is relevant to note that teletandem participants are not expected to know how to explain linguistic norms and rules because they are native (or proficient) speakers – not language teachers. However, because this participant was enrolled in a language teacher education undergraduate program, she probably felt that she should have known how to explain 'relative clauses', a topic which had been taught in one of the face-to-face lessons. The student is actually focusing on her (lack of) abilities to explain the grammar topic. The teacher's comment (question) seems an attempt to (1) offer support in relation to a difficulty that is related to her competence to become a foreign language teacher, (2) foster the learner's reflection on what he/she learned (or not) about a linguistic topic that was focused on in the face-to-face lesson. At the same time, the teacher may get information on how effective that specific lesson might have been, which is in accordance with Black and Wiliam's (1998) proposal that classroom assessment should inform both teaching and learning.

Figure 6 reveals the learner's struggles in dealing with social and physical distancing rules that should be obeyed due to the COVID19 pandemic in 2020.

Figure 6. 2020_USA_diary01[10]

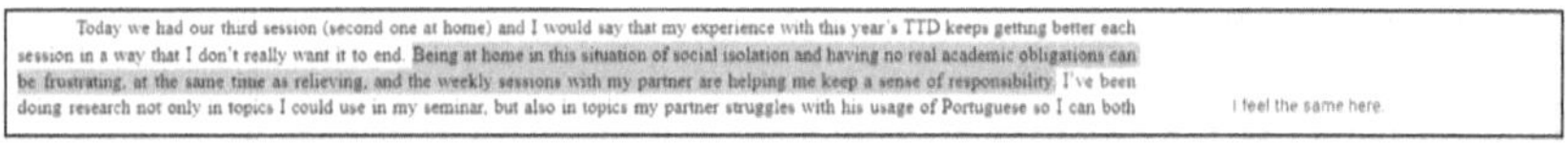

> Today we had our third session (second one at home) and I would say that my experience with this year's TTD keeps getting better each session in a way that I don't really want it to end. Being at home in this situation of social isolation and having no real academic obligations can be frustrating, at the same time as relieving, and the weekly sessions with my partner are helping me keep a sense of responsibility. I've been doing research not only in topics I could use in my seminar, but also in topics my partner struggles with his usage of Portuguese so I can both   *I feel the same here.*

---

9. Our translation to the sentence the teacher selects to add the feedback to: Which - the non restrictive element is a word, phrase or clause related to excessive information in the beginning of a sentence without restricting the meaning of the sentence. A more readable version of this figure can be viewed online in supplementary materials.

10. A more readable version of this figure can be viewed online in supplementary materials.

Even though this difficulty is not particularly related to the teletandem setting, the feedback is intended to show the learner that she is not 'alone' and reveals that the teacher acknowledges the crucial role that affective factors play in the telecollaborative learning process, as widely studied in face-to-face contexts as well.

3.3. Feedback related to linguistic (in)accuracies

When the diaries are written in English, teachers focus on linguistic inadequacies and suggest the revision of some words or stretches of text. They sometimes use the comment box to give hints on what should be revised (see Figure 7).

Figure 7. 2016_UK_diary04

> Today my partner is not very well, she told me that she got a sick and that she got hangover too. We start the conversation in English because she thought that she couldn't speak a good portuguese today. We discuss her essay, and I told her that it is much more portuguese of Portugal than portuguese of Brazil. With her essay I learn two new things in portuguese, first of all a realise how we, Brazilians, use too much the gerund when I correct this sentence "Quando estava a viver em Coimbra" to this one "Quando estava vivendo em Coimbra". Another thing is that she uses "cá em Inglaterra" and I just correct for "aqui na Inglaterra" because I thought that was strange. Then I search that there is a difference between "cá" and "aqui" and I found that so interesting.
>
> 31 de out. de 2016 — sick is an adjective
> 31 de out. de 2016 — tense
> 31 de out. de 2016 — countable and capital letter

In other cases, they use the 'suggesting edits' feature of Google Docs, which allows students to track the changes made to the file and accept them or not (see Figure 8).

Figure 8. 2016_UK_diary01

> My partner, ██, is very cute. She started the conversation saying hi and everything in Pportuguese. She surprised me, because my last partners have-always beguninning with English and she seems so excited tospeak talk in Pportuguese. First we discussed my text and she had corrected and explained all my errors so we didn't have much things to discuss, we just argued about some sentences that were "aportuguesadas"(Portuguese-like_ and she doesn't didn't understand what I wanted to say.

Chapter 4

It is relevant to note that this teacher's 'suggestions' are a revision strategy that leaves space for learners' decisions on what (or if) they want to change in their own diary entries. Revising the learners' diaries in terms of linguistic inaccuracies may seem at 'odds' with the purpose of the diary, which is to foster reflection. However, since the feedback is individualized and private, it is not likely to threaten learners' faces and it can inform them about linguistic aspects that must be improved.

All these instances of feedback are considered 'asynchronous moments of contingency' in which teachers try to support the individual student's learning process. Whereas asynchronous moments are present in every comment, diaries may also serve to feed the synchronous moments of contingency, i.e. group discussions in face-to-face lessons. As teachers give feedback, they collect the most recurrent and/or relevant issues in a separate file called 'mediation sessions'.

Figure 9. 2020_USA_teacher's file

> Session 1: issues to be discussed
> - Making the other learn words in their own language (condominium) and the differences of housing.
> - Cultural comparisons: astonishment with the fact that strikes also happen in England.
> - How do you see the fact that "Because this was the first interaction, we didn't have activities to do, so we just discussed things and fun facts about random people"?

Figure 9 indicates that the asynchronous one-to-one feedback assists teachers' planning and contributes to the synchronous group discussion. This, in turn, may help teachers create a coherent whole as they establish links between what is done in the VE and what is done in face-to-face lessons. This seems to be in accordance with Black and Wiliam (2009), who propose that these two moments of contingency should have the purpose to inform the teaching-learning process.

4. Conclusions and lessons learned

Feedback to participants' diaries allows teachers to assess not only what students say they are (not) learning, but also what they are struggling with and how they feel about the challenges they are facing. Besides, when diaries are written in English, feedback can focus on language and reveal both the teacher and the student some learning gaps on linguistic development. While teachers establish a private, one-to-one, asynchronous dialogue with individual learners, they also collect relevant information to be discussed in mediation sessions. As challenging and time-consuming reading all the learners' diaries on a weekly basis may be, this formative assessment practice allows teachers to follow students' autonomous and collaborative work and to make informed decisions about the language teaching-learning process, which are crucial aspects of meaningful integration of telecollaborative practice and face-to-face lessons. It should be noted, however, that this type of formative assessment is not guided by pre-established rubrics. Feedback seems to be based on the knowledge the teacher has of each individual student and of the specificities of the learning setting. In this sense, feedback on learners' diaries seem to open a window for the teacher to (1) contemplate the individual's achievements; (2) understand the accomplishment of the different VE tasks by each learner, and (3) establish connections with the broader pedagogical objectives of the EFL program.

5. Supplementary materials

https://research-publishing.box.com/s/i4ios0jfijhbvkke6wz1h5gqsfpv9gzb

References

Aranha, S., & Cavalari, S. M. S. (2014). A trajetória do projeto Teletandem Brasil: da modalidade institucional não-integrada à institucional integrada. *The especialist, 35*(2).

Aranha, S., & Cavalari, S. M. S. (2021). Teletandem. *Panorama da contribuição do Brasil para a difusão do português – Brasília*, 321-328.

Aranha, S., & Leone, P. (2017). The development of DOTI (data of oral teletandem interaction). Investigating computer-mediated communication: corpus-based approaches to language in the digital world. *Ljubljana: University of Ljubljana, Faculty of Arts, 1*, 172-192.

Black, P., & Wiliam, D. (1998). Assessment and classroom learning. *Assessment in Education: principles, policy & practice, 5*(1), 7-74. https://doi.org/10.1080/0969595980050102

Black, P., & Wiliam, D. (2009). Developing the theory of formative assessment. *Educational Assessment, Evaluation and Accountability (formerly: Journal of Personnel Evaluation in Education), 21*(1), 5-31. https://doi.org/10.1007/s11092-008-9068-5

Brammerts, H. (1996). Language learning in tandem using the Internet. *Telecollaboration in foreign language learning*, 121-130.

Cavalari, S. M. S., & Aranha, S. (2016). Teletandem: integrating e-learning into the foreign language classroom. *Acta Scientiarum: Language and Culture, 38*(4), 327-336. https://doi.org/10.4025/actascilangcult.v38i4.28139

Cavalari, S. M. S., & Aranha, S. (2019). The teacher's role in telecollaborative language learning: the case of institutional integrated teletandem. *Revista Brasileira de Lnguística Aplicada, 19*, 555-578. https://doi.org/10.1590/1984-6398201913576

Levet, S. (2015). The cultura model: developing students' intercultural competence. *FLTMAG*. https://fltmag.com/the-cultura-model/

Moon, J. (2010). *Learning journals and logs*. Centre for Teaching and Learning, UCD Dublin. http://www.deakin.edu.au/itl/assets/resources/pd/tl-modules/teaching-approach/group-assignments/learning-journals.pdf

Sadler, R., & Dooly, M. (2016). Twelve years of telecollaboration: what we have learnt. *ELT Journal, 70*(4), 401-413. https://doi.org/10.1093/elt/ccw041

Telles, J. A. (2006). *Teletandem Brasil: Línguas Estrangeiras para todos*. Research Project.

Telles, J. A., & Vassallo, M. L. (2006). Foreign language learning in-tandem: teletandem as an alternative proposal in CALLT. *The ESPecialist, 27*(2), 189-212.

5. Peer group mediation sessions as an assessment tool in teletandem

Anna-Katharina Elstermann[1]

Abstract

The purpose of this chapter is to present peer group mediation as one of the assessment practices within Teletandem Brasil, a Virtual Exchange (VE) project which uses tandem practice between university students of different countries for foreign language learning, carried out through videoconferencing tools. Peer group mediation sessions are regular meetings, in addition to the teletandem practice, and aim at promoting reflection on telecollaborative, intercultural, and language learning, and individual learning processes. Assessment is seen here as a practice by students, mediators, and peers that seeks to reflect upon and respond to information from dialogue, demonstration, and observation in ways that enhance ongoing learning.

Keywords: peer group mediation, teletandem, assessment.

1. Introduction

In this chapter, I will present the VE project *Teletandem Brasil* and one of the forms of assessment used to evaluate language learning of the participants of the project. Teletandem is a learning context based on mutual language exchange between learning partners where each learner is a native

---

1. Writing Centre of Goethe-Universität, Frankfurt, Germany; elstermann@em.uni-frankfurt.de; https://orcid.org/0000-0002-5430-972X

How to cite: Elstermann, A.-K. (2022). Peer group mediation sessions as an assessment tool in teletandem. In A. Czura & M. Dooly (Eds), *Assessing virtual exchange in foreign language courses at tertiary level* (pp. 79-91). Research-publishing.net. https://doi.org/10.14705/rpnet.2022.59.1411

or proficient speaker in the language the other wants to learn. One of the assessment forms used in this VE project is called 'peer group mediation'. Peer group mediation consists of regular peer meetings in which learners discuss and reflect on their learning of foreign languages and cultures. This form of assessment departs from what assessment is commonly thought of, i.e. summative assessment, ranking, tests, or grades, etc. For this reason, I prefer to use a broader parameter of assessment, the so called *assessment FOR learning* and *assessment OF learning.* Broadfoot et al. (2002) defined assessment FOR learning as "the process of seeking and interpreting evidence for use by learners and their teachers to decide where the learners are in their learning, where they need to go and how best to get there" (pp. 2-3). Assessment for learning is any assessment whose first priority in its design and practice is to serve the purpose of promoting students' learning. Thus, it differs from assessment OF learning designed primarily to serve the purposes of accountability, ranking, or certifying competence (Wiliam, 2011). Assessment for learning, therefore, is part of everyday practice by students, teachers, and peers who aim to seek, reflect upon, and respond to information from dialogue, demonstration, and observation in ways that enhance ongoing learning (Klenowski, 2009).

In the teletandem context, thus, assessment is not testing for summative purposes. Assessment in teletandem is a practice that faces all the challenges of providing a learning awareness tool which can also be useful for research purposes. These peculiarities are intrinsic to the teletandem context in the view of the fact that teletandem participants are immersed in an autonomous, telecollaborative, and intercultural learning environment fuelled by constant research activities. Therefore, project coordinators and mediators use peer group mediation sessions to promote reflection on and discussion about language learning and, simultaneously, to gain a little insight into where the learners are in their learning processes. The learning and improvement of a foreign language is not the only aspect emphasised in teletandem. Participants are also introduced to means for improving their attitudinal skills for autonomous learning, learning strategies, and their intercultural competence; all topics addressed during peer group mediation.

The term 'mediation' as a form of learner support in teletandem draws upon Vygotsky's (1991) work, in particular his concepts of mediation: the Zone of Proximal Development (ZPD) and scaffolding (Elstermann, 2017)[2].

> "The basis of Vygotsky's theory is that culture has a profound influence on how humans think; the relation between human beings and their world around them is not direct [rather it is] mediated by culture and society" (Lantolf & Poehner, 2011, p. 11, cited in Elstermann, 2017, p. 104).

The ZPD is understood as the distance between the actual level of development of a learner and their potential level of development. This potential level of development is identified by the learner's problem solving capacity under guidance of (or mediated by) an adult or in collaboration with a more capable peer (Vygotsky, 1991). That is why the mediator in teletandem plays an important role in the learning process as s/he selects and sets the experiences that lead to learning (providing the guidance or scaffolding adequate for the ZPD). For Salomão (2011, p. 659), the mediation sessions in teletandem help participants reflect on their own practice as language learners and teachers of their own language. According to her, the mediator in teletandem is closely linked to the conceptualisation of knowledge construction in Vygotsky's social theory of knowledge, which places emphasis on its development through social interaction, which inevitably includes language use.

In the following sections of this chapter, I will present in more detail the *Teletandem Brasil* project and the concept of peer group mediation as a form of assessment for foreign language and intercultural learning within this VE project.

---

2. Many works on learner support in language learning use the terms 'advising' or 'counselling' which derive from theories like Carl Rogers's approach of person-centred counselling or cognitive behavioural therapy (cf. Brammerts & Kleppin, 2001; Carson & Mynard, 2012; Claußen, 2009).

Chapter 5

2. Overview of the project *Teletandem Brasil*

The VE project *Teletandem Brasil – Línguas Estrangeiras para todos* at the Brazilian public university *Universidade Estadual Paulista* (UNESP) offers tandem[3] language exchange via videoconferencing tools such as *Skype*, *Google Meet*, or *Zoom* for Brazilian L2 students with partner universities around the world. It is based on the principles of autonomy, reciprocity, and separation of languages (Vassallo & Telles, 2009).

The project was created by Telles and Vassallo in 2006/2007 as a response to the necessity to offer authentic communication situations with native or competent speakers of different foreign languages for their students enrolled in language teacher training courses. Due to geographical reasons, tandem had not been popular in Brazil. However, with the advent of new communication technologies and broadband internet, Brazilian L2 students had the possibility to work collaboratively with native speakers around the world. At that time, this was a significant innovation in the field of teaching and learning of foreign languages in Brazil (Elstermann, 2017).

The *Teletandem Brasil* project started with four partner universities from the USA, Germany, France, and Italy. Today, the project is established on three campuses with specific teletandem computer labs hosting up to 150 hours of teletandem activities and 15 university partnerships per semester. Each semester, the coordinating teams of the teletandem project on each campus organise the activities for the current semester. This involves opening the enrollment for each teletandem group, accompanying the ongoing teletandem activities, guiding the mediation sessions, and supervising the final evaluation of each group. One teletandem group has a semester-long exchange with another group of learners of a foreign university. They conduct between four to ten sessions per semester.

---

3. "The tandem learning context consists of several main characteristics including: (a) the collaboration of two learners (with individual learning goals but one goal in common: to help each other in the learning process), (b) the use of two different languages, (c) reciprocity, and (d) autonomy" (Elstermann, 2017, p. 30). As defined by Little (1991), "tandem language learning is a form of open learning in which two people with different mother tongues work together in order to learn one another's language" (p. 1). "This pair of learners usually agrees on meeting at regular intervals with at least the common goal of learning each other's language, exchanging personal, cultural and linguistic information and sometimes even information about academic or professional activities" (Elstermann, 2017, p. 28).

One session usually has a duration of 60 minutes, 25 minutes for each language and ten minutes for peer feedback. The teletandem sessions are followed by mediation sessions of about 30 minutes, which focus on linguistic and cultural aspects, the student's learning process, and issues that emerge from teletandem interactions (Telles, 2015).

The main group of participants of this VE project are university students enrolled in foreign language teacher training courses. Exceptionally, students from other university courses as well as the academic staff can also participate.

The main objectives of the VE project are the promotion of autonomous foreign language learning, with the focus on training and gaining more oral and intercultural competences. Since teletandem is a learner autonomy promoting context, the creation and execution of specific learning tasks are not the focus of the project, i.e. there is no creation or compilation of specific exercises for the teletandem project. Nevertheless, many of the participating language teachers opt to give a task for each teletandem session in order to help their students find a conversation topic or even to prepare homework for the respective language course in which the students are participating. Those tasks usually aim to get information about cultural themes such as a specific holiday, festivities, regional food and drink, etc. Some teachers, in fact, prepare a list of conversation topics.

3. Peer group mediation as assessment for learning

Besides the actual teletandem sessions, the mediation sessions, as briefly mentioned in the previous section, have become an integral part of the *Teletandem Brasil* project. In this section, the peer group mediation sessions are described in more detail, however, depending on the partner university and individual arrangements between teachers, coordinators, and mediators, the forms of assessment can vary (see the chapter of Cavalari & Aranha, 2022, on learners' diaries in teletandem, this volume).

With one exception, the teletandem project has not been included in the curricula of foreign language studies; it continues to be considered an extracurricular activity with neither credits nor grades given for performance or participation in the project. Thus, participants only receive a certificate of participation if they attend regularly. Since no grades or credits are required institutionally, there is no need for testing specific learning outcomes. Nevertheless, different forms of assessment have been used since the beginning of the project to collect data for research projects and for the purposes of internal evaluations. In addition to mediation sessions, reflective diaries or journals (see Cavalari & Aranha, 2022, this volume; Evangelista & Salomão, 2019), discussion forums on Moodle, Teleduc, closed Facebook groups (Garcia & Souza, 2018), most recently, Whatsapp groups (Campos, Kami, & Salomão, 2021), and text productions with peer feedback and teacher feedback (Aranha & Cavalari, 2014) have been used. In this section, the focus will be on peer group mediation sessions (Elstermann, 2017).

Within the *Teletandem Brasil* project, mediation became an essential part of the process of teaching and learning languages, since the learners alone may not be able to explore the whole potential of their learning context. Evangelista and Salomão (2019) argue that the mediation sessions help learners to better understand the teletandem sessions, to understand that it is more than just an act of talking. Through the mediation sessions, learners have access to guided reflection about the learning context that opens up possibilities to enhance their linguistic, intercultural, and autonomous learning. The mediator, thus, has the role of guiding the learners to reflect on language, culture, strategies, and approaches to teaching and learning and support them in their difficulties encountered during the learning process (Garcia, 2015; Salomão, 2011; Souza, Zakir, & Garcia, 2021).

In a previous study (Elstermann, 2017), I tried to compile the characteristics of peer group mediation for language learning in telecollaborative projects such as teletandem. According to the research findings, the **main objective** of peer group mediation is the promotion of reflection on issues concerning intercultural and language learning, given that they are the main pillars of the learning context in teletandem. Other **specific objectives** include reflection on learning strategies and tactics, on evaluation of the learning process, on the principles of tandem learning (autonomy, reciprocity, and language use), and especially on the exchange of ideas, difficulties, questions, and experiences between the participating peers (Elstermann, 2017, p. 336).

Peer group mediation can be realised in face-to-face **settings**, at university. In this case, only one side of the learners take part in the mediation session. When peer group mediation is held virtually via videoconferencing tools, one or both sides can participate. In terms of the **frequency** of the mediation sessions, they occur on a regular basis, usually once a week or biweekly. There are two possibilities for the realisation of the peer group mediation sessions:

- if the teletandem is carried out through the autonomous modality and learners are doing their teletandem sessions from home at individually set dates and hours, meetings are held regularly (biweekly or with even longer intervals) for approximately one hour; and

- if teletandem is done institutionally in a semi or fully integrated modality (i.e. in group settings in the computer lab of the university at specific dates and hours in a weekly rhythm), the peer group mediation sessions are held directly after the interactions are finished, for approximately 30 minutes.

The use of **different communication or data collection tools** for the mediation sessions is possible. Mediator's notes and some online platforms such as Moodle or Google Classroom for asynchronous discussion between the peers and the mediator and for information-giving are the tools which are mostly commonly used (Elstermann, 2017, p. 337). Other options are learner biographies, learner diaries, questionnaires, and videos or transcripts of recorded teletandem sessions in order to discuss examples of practice in the mediation session.

Concerning **the use of language** for discussion and reflection in the mediation session, there are different approaches (Funo, 2015), and it is usually the mediator who decides on the use of the language. If the mediator wishes to use the mediation sessions for extra foreign language training, s/he may choose the foreign language that was used throughout the teletandem practice. If the main objective of the mediation session is to reflect upon individual learning processes and strategies, the first language (L1) of the teletandem participants may be a better choice. Data showed that discussions on meta-language, culture, and learning processes were difficult when the foreign language competencies were B1 or below (Elstermann, 2017).

Regarding the actual **procedure** of a regular in-class mediation session, the process is as below.

- All participants sit in a circle. An open and friendly atmosphere is important for learners' participation.

- The mediator initiates the mediation session with a more general and open question about the teletandem sessions in order to help the students begin their reflection on their experience during the teletandem session. The usual initial questions/ice breakers are: *What moment do you remember most from your teletandem session today?*, *What topic was most on your minds in your session today?*, and *Who would like to share a funny moment from his/her today's session?*.

- Participants respond to the initial question and usually a conversation and exchange spins out of it.

- The mediator continuously analyses the comments and responses from the learners to subsequently underline or reinforce one of the topics mentioned. Usually the participants have numerous experiences to share and appreciate the exchange of information and learning experiences.

- We suggest that the mediator be prepared for initiating reflection upon topics such as (1) cultural stereotypes, (2) cultural prejudices, (3) the other and I (foreign culture versus the own culture), (4) transculturality, interculturality, and cross/multiculturality, and (5) awareness of sensitive topics such as politics, religion, race, and sexuality.

- The mediator should take notes on the topics addressed in the mediation session as well on the comments of the learners that seem important to him/her.

- When the end of the mediation session approaches, the mediator guides the discussion to an end. Eventually s/he gives suggestions for 'homework reflection' until the next meeting. The mediator should reflect again on the contents of the mediation session and prepare future discussions and reflections based on what was mentioned or commented on by the participants.

Through joint and partly guided reflection and discussion on learning foreign languages, aspects of their own and the other culture and, if necessary, linguistic difficulties, the peers give each other feedback and assistance, which in turn promotes and expands the linguistic, intercultural, and learning competencies of all participants. The mediator gains an overview of where the participants stand, what their beliefs are about language, culture, and their learning processes, and can return to aspects that s/she feels need further deepening in subsequent mediation sessions by further addressing specific topics and questions.

4. Conclusions and lessons learnt

In this chapter I presented peer group mediation sessions as a form of assessment aimed at accompanying learners in their autonomous learning process of foreign languages and cultures in teletandem. The importance here is to observe and evaluate learners' reflections upon their own learning and upon their own conversations with their foreign learning partners.

Several studies on mediation sessions proved that the discussions and reflections between the peers are enriching, can promote intercultural awareness and learner autonomy, and even provide chances to enhance language competences (Elstermann, 2017; Evangelista & Salomão, 2019; Funo, 2015; Garcia & Souza, 2018, to mention a few). The sharing and exchange of the learning experiences of their teletandem partnerships help the peers to reflect on their own learning in a deeper way and to get more ideas for their own teletandem practice. Furthermore, the discussions on intercultural aspects proved to be crucial for the deconstruction of stereotypes and prejudices in relation to the foreign culture. The latter aspect is also one of the challenges in the project. International telecollaboration projects seem to be perfect contexts for promoting intercultural competence. However, Telles (2015) and Messias and Telles (2020) observed that the conversations held during the teletandem practice can often reinforce stereotypes and prejudices in terms of linguistic and cultural aspects. Therefore, it is one of the tasks of the mediator to guide the discussion in mediation sessions in a way that learners become more sensitive and open to intercultural aspects and begin the process of reflecting on language and culture in a less traditional, dichotomous way.

The role of the mediator cannot be underestimated, as it is a multi-faceted and complex role (Elstermann, 2017). The mediator should have experience in the processes of foreign language learning and teaching, inter/transcultural issues, and counselling skills such as active listening, focusing, and summarising for instance, and in the case of the teletandem project, should also be acquainted with the project itself. To assure a minimum of mediation competence, it is advisable to offer a mediator training for those who are interested in becoming one. In projects with the focus on language learning, mediators often are language teachers, graduate students, or more experienced undergraduate students. Within the *Teletandem Brasil* project, the coordinators launched the first mediator training in 2012 due to the increasing number of teletandem interactions and the need for more mediators to attend the interactions. The mediator training consisted in four meetings to present and discuss topics, including concepts of learner autonomy, language learning in teletandem, learning strategies, and a practical part in which the participating students had to shadow a teacher-mediator at a mediation session (Funo & Elstermann, 2012). The training structure and contents have been regularly adapted to meet new demands, especially since the start of the COVID-19 pandemic (see Campos et al., 2021; Souza et al., 2021). A more extensive research about mediator training in VE projects such as *Teletandem Brasil* and the development of an asynchronous training course for mediators is currently being created by Camila Kami (in progress).

Peer group mediation sessions as a form of assessment certainly may be used in other contexts and for other VE projects. The main characteristics of peer group mediation such as the setting, frequency, tools, and procedure can be easily adapted to other target groups. As the main idea of the mediation sessions is to share experiences and jointly reflect and discuss, there are no restrictions regarding the content, i.e. it need not be a language exchange project; it could have any focus whatsoever. The most important and interesting aspect behind this kind of assessment is that it promotes ongoing learning, it does not merely test or grade a learning outcome.

Recommended readings

www.teletandembrasil.org

References

Aranha, S., & Cavalari, S. (2014). A trajetória do projeto Teletandem Brasil: da modalidade institucional não-integrada à institucional integrada. *The ESPecialist, São Paulo, 35*(2), 183-201.

Brammerts, H., & Kleppin, K. (2001). (Eds). *Selbstgesteuertes Sprachenlernen im Tandem*. Stauffenburg Verlag.

Broadfoot, P. M., Daugherty, R., Gardner, J., Harlen, W., James, M., & Stobart, G. (2002). *Assessment for learning: 10 principles*. University of Cambridge School of Education.

Campos, B., Kami, C., & Salomão, A. (2021). A mediação no Teletandem durante a pandemia da COVID-19. *Revista Horizontes de Linguística Aplicada, Brasília, 20*(1), DT3.

Carson, L., & Mynard, J. (2012). Introduction. In J. Mynard & L. Carson (Eds), *Advising in language learning* (pp. 3-25). Pearson Education.

Cavalari, S., & Aranha, S. (2022). Learners' diaries as a tool for teachers' assessment in teletandem. In A. Czura & M. Dooly (Eds), *Assessing virtual exchange in foreign language courses at tertiary level* (pp. 65-78). Research-publishing.net. https://doi.org/10.14705/rpnet.2022.59.1410

Claußen, T. (2009). *Strategientraining und Lernberatung*. Stauffenburg.

Elstermann, A. (2017). *Learner support in telecollaboration: peer group mediation in teletandem*. Ruhr-Universität.

Evangelista, M., & Salomão, A. (2019). Mediation in teletandem: from face-to-face sessions to reflective journals. *Pandaemonium, São Paulo, 22*(36), 153-177. https://doi.org/10.11606/1982-88372236153

Funo, L. (2015). *Teletandem: um estudo sobre identidades culturais e sessões de mediação em aprendizagem*. PhD Dissertation. Universidade Estadual Paulista, Brazil.

Funo, L., & Elstermann, A. (2012). *Aprendizagem de Línguas em Teletandem*. Poster presentation at I JELT.

Garcia, D. (2015). A logística das sessões de interação e mediação no teletandem com vistas ao ensino/aprendizagem de línguas estrangeiras. *Estudos Linguísticos, São Paulo, 44*(2), 725-738.

Garcia, D., & Souza, M. (2018). Teletandem mediation on Facebook. *Revista do GEL, São Paulo, 15*(3), 155-175. https://doi.org/10.21165/gel.v15i3.2400

Kami, C. (in progress). *Formação de mediadores de Teletandem*. PhD Dissertation. Universidade Estadual Paulista, Brazil.

Klenowski, V. (2009). Editorial. Assessment for learning revisited: an Asia-Pacific perspective. *Assessment in Education: Principles, Policy, and Practice, 16*(3), 263-268. https://doi.org/10.1080/09695940903319646

Lantolf, J. P., & Poehner, M. E. (2011). *Dynamic assessment in the foreign language classroom: a teacher's guide* (2nd ed.). CALPER publications.

Little, D. (1991). *Learner autonomy: definitions, issues and problems*. Authentik.

Messias, R., & Telles, J. (2020). Teletandem como "terceiro espaço" no desenvolvimento de professores de línguas estrangeiras. *ETD – Educação Temática Digital, Campinas, SP, 22*(3), 731-750. https://doi.org/10.20396/etd.v22i3.8655293

Salomão, A. (2011). A formação do formador de professores: perspectivas de colaboração entre graduandos e pós-graduandos no projeto Teletandem Brasil. *Revista Brasileira de Linguística Aplicada, 11*(3), 653-677. https://doi.org/10.1590/S1984-63982011000300004

Souza, M., Zakir, M., & Garcia, D. (2021). An overview of teletandem mediation courses for teacher education. *DELTA*, 37(1), 1-24. https://doi.org/10.1590/1678-460x2021370107

Telles, J. A. (2015). Learning foreign languages in teletandem: resources and strategies. *DELTA*, *31*(3), 651-680. https://doi.org/10.1590/0102-4450226475643730772

Vassallo, M. L., & Telles, J. A. (2009). Ensino e aprendizagem de línguas em tandem: princípios teóricos e perspectivas de pesquisa. In J. A. Telles (Ed.), *Teletandem: um contexto virtual, autônomo e colaborativo para aprendizagem de línguas estrangeiras no século XXI* (pp. 21-42). Pontes Editores.

Vygotsky, L. S. (1991). *A formação social da mente*. Martins Fontes.

Wiliam, D. (2011). What is assessment for learning? *Studies in Educational Evaluation, 37*(1), 3-14. https://doi.org/10.1016/j.stueduc.2011.03.001

6 Peer assessment of process writing in a virtual exchange project

Anna Czura[1] and Agnieszka M. Sendur[2]

Abstract

One of the possible ways of assessing students' collaborative work in Virtual Exchange (VE) is by the use of Peer Assessment (PA) – a formative assessment technique in which students review each other's work to provide descriptive feedback on the basis of a set of criteria. This article describes a VE procedure, in which students from three different institutions collaborate on the preparation of a tourist brochure. The project participants include two European English for tourism classes and a group of native-speaker participants of an English composition class at a US university. The proposed VE scheme is supplemented with a possible PA procedure and evaluation criteria that has been developed on the basis of previous VE experiences, the students' post-project feedback, and the subject literature.

Keywords: peer assessment, foreign language learning, formative assessment, virtual exchange.

1. Introduction

One of the defining features of VE is collaboration, which involves working with other peers both from the home and the partner institutions towards a common

---

1. Universitat Autònoma de Barcelona, Barcelona, Spain; anna.czura@uwr.edu.pl; https://orcid.org/0000-0001-5234-6618

2. Andrzej Frycz Modrzewski Krakow University, Krakow, Poland; asendur@afm.edu.pl; https://orcid.org/0000-0001-8245-1427

How to cite: Czura, A., & Sendur, A. M. (2022). Peer assessment of process writing in a virtual exchange project. In A. Czura & M. Dooly (Eds), *Assessing virtual exchange in foreign language courses at tertiary level* (pp. 93-106). Research-publishing.net. https://doi.org/10.14705/rpnet.2022.59.1412

goal. The collaborative learning can also be reflected in the assessment process through the use of PA, during which students provide each other feedback on the basis of a set of clearly defined criteria. PA is inherently linked with the idea of learner autonomy and learner-centred education, in which the teacher transfers some part of control to the students, who, in turn, need to assume a certain degree of responsibility for their own learning.

As a part of formative assessment (also termed as *assessment for learning*), PA engages students in the process of co-creating assessment criteria and providing feedback to each other. As Little and Perclová (2001) observe, the ability to use assessment criteria in practice can bring far-reaching benefits as it helps students understand standards of both in-class and high-stakes assessments. Moreover, by assessing others, students learn how to apply the standards to reflect on the quality of their own work and, thus, develop self-assessment skills. Assessing peers' work based on clearly articulated criteria encourages students to make decisions, analyse, and reason, which also contributes to their cognitive development and critical thinking skills (Cheng & Warren, 2005). Additionally, some studies show that learners prefer to receive critical remarks from their peers rather than from the teacher (Black et al., 2003) and consider them more motivating and useful (Czura, 2016; Peng, 2010). Deakin-Crick et al. (2005) add that the value of PA lies in the fact that the students offer each other feedback using more approachable language and feel free to ask other students questions they would otherwise feel inhibited to ask.

Critics of PA point out that students with a low level of linguistic competence are not able to correct other students' mistakes. It must be noted, however, that this form of assessment does not only refer to linguistic correctness, but can also include an array of other criteria, such as content, structure, or very specific language-related aspects described and explained in detail prior to PA. As Cheng and Warren (2005) indicate, PA and teacher assessment of the same work may produce different results. This should not be approached as a drawback as these two forms of evaluation have different objectives; PA has a predominantly formative function based on providing feedback according to assessment criteria, whereas teachers' assessments, especially in an institutionalised context, often need to be supplemented with a formal grade. The main merit of PA lies in the fact that it enables students to analyse each other's work and provide descriptive feedback according to previously established standards (Brown & Abeywickrama, 2019).

Since PA is embedded in the social context and, thus, may evoke specific cognitive and emotional reactions, introduction of this form of assessment should be treated as a multi-stage process for which students should be gradually prepared. It is particularly important in contexts where students are not used to working autonomously, without teachers' direct supervision (cf. Czura & Baran-Łucarz, 2021; Verzella & Sendur, 2019). Research also suggests that students benefit from such a scaffolded approach, and the quality of the feedback they provide increases as they gain more experience (e.g. Sluijsmans, Brand-Gruwel, & Van Merriënboer, 2002). Gielen and De Wever (2015) underscore "the need for structure and support to ensure effective feedback" (p. 437), which can be achieved when peer feedback is based on a list of clearly defined assessment criteria and aims to provide answers to three major questions proposed by Hattie and Timperley (2007): "Where am I going?", "How am I going?", and "Where to next?" (p. 88). The assessment criteria can be provided in the form of peer checklists, categorical scales, or selected curriculum requirements. The specific design of the PA procedure needs to take into account, among others, the educational context in which it takes place, course objectives, group dynamics, students' prior experience, task type, content, and, in the case of VE, additionally the mode of communication and language(s) used.

PA can be easily incorporated into task design, and often one can find its application as an assessment tool in VE projects to support collaborative language learning (e.g. Dooly & Sadler, 2019; Van de Kraak & Lai, 2020; Vinagre & Muñoz, 2011). PA tools typically involve rubrics, checklists, corrective comments, and written reports; however, they can be adapted to match more specific objectives of a VE project. For instance, in their VE project that involved elements of gamification, Sevilla-Pavón and Haba-Osca (2017) used PA "in the form of votes in assessment rubrics and voting polls for digital stories [...] and oral presentations" and written "investors' reports" as a part of a larger reward system that was concluded with "an award ceremony" (p. 244). Additionally, online tools such as TEAMMATES (Dooly, 2022, this volume) and Wooclap (Vuylsteke, 2022, this volume) enable smooth implementation of PA among all distanced partners, offering feedback that is immediately available to both students and teachers.

Regardless of the form and mode of PA, it is prerogative that students receive appropriate training and guidelines that would help them provide feedback to each other on different aspects of learning in a constructive and non-threatening manner (for an example of a project preparing students for giving and receiving online peer feedback see Ennis et al., 2021). On the basis of their study, Ware and O'Dowd (2008) underline the role of teacher's scaffolding: "Instructors must not only make clear their expectations that students provide feedback, but they must also provide examples of when and how to provide feedback" (p. 56). To this end, in their course focused on developing linguistic accuracy and complexity through VE, Ware and Cañado (2007) put forward a set of sample guidelines on language-related and interpersonal interactional strategies that can help students formulate efficient and meaningful feedback.

There are ample studies that show that PA can benefit the learning process in a VE project. This chapter does not showcase the whole assessment process in a VE, but rather presents a step-by-step approach to introducing PA. The procedure has evolved as a result of previous VE projects involving students of tourism from Italy and Poland, and American students of English composition. The first-hand experience of the past VE projects, the participants' opinions about the collaborative writing, US students' feedback to the received drafts (for details see Verzella & Sendur, 2019), and a thorough review of subject literature helped us to take a critical look, by observing the strong points as well as the shortcomings of the previous exchanges and student outputs. The PA procedure was modified accordingly with a view to providing the students with better support throughout the process, facilitating closer intercultural dialogue and improving the consistency of peer feedback. In the next section, we delineate and reflect on the redesigned PA procedure, which, in our view, addresses to a greater degree the needs of students in our educational context. Some concrete examples of assessment criteria are also provided.

2. Overview of the VE project

The original VE project involved three groups from three different countries – two groups of English for tourism (EfT) students at two European universities and a group of native speakers from an American university. The group from Poland, taught by the second author, consisted of undergraduate students of tourism and recreation at the Andrzej Frycz Modrzewski Krakow University. The English as a foreign language/English for specific purposes course aimed at developing the students' general language skills to a B2 level, and equipping them with the necessary EfT language. The second European group made up of students completing a master's degree in heritage and tourism at the University of Molise, Italy, attended a EfT class with similar objectives to that of the group based in Poland. The third group consisted of native English speakers enrolled in an obligatory English composition class at North Dakota State University, US. This course aimed to help students develop their writing skills in a variety of genres for different audiences, and to come to see writing as a collaborative and negotiated process.

On the linguistic level, the VE project was designed to enable students to use English as a global lingua franca, which entails "linguistic, rhetorical, and cultural common grounds" (Verzella & Sendur, 2019, p. 171) and acquaint them with the principles of persuasive writing that may be of use in their future professional activity. Additionally, given the interactive and international nature of the project, it was also intended to encourage students' reflection on the importance of intercultural competence.

The main student output was a travel brochure advertising a selected region or a tourist attraction addressed to young, college-educated international tourists. This was supposed to be written in a persuasive language and illustrated with appropriate visual aids. Following Dudley-Evans and St John's (1998) recommendation, the teachers adopted the synthesis of the product and process approaches to writing. Accordingly, the collaborative writing started with a presentation and detailed analysis of model texts. Then, working towards the final product, the students produced several drafts on the basis of the comments received from their peers (for more detailed analysis of the VE project see Verzella & Sendur, 2019).

In the post-project discussions, the students and the partnering instructors came to the conclusion that notwithstanding all the values the VE brought into our courses, there had been some flaws in the design and planning that needed reconsidering for future use. We all agreed that the project was too long and too complicated. The continuing and repetitive character of the tasks (too many rounds of peer feedback), as well as their complexity (the students had to prepare their own brochures, comment on their peers' work, analyse, assess, and make use of the comments provided by the reviewers and introduce appropriate revisions) brought about the feeling of weariness and a longing for the task to come to an end. The students from the European universities also complained about the lack of opportunity for more direct contact with the partners due to the asynchronous nature of the project. Another drawback was an incomplete understanding of the assessment criteria. Although the Polish and the Italian groups had been given a set of guiding questions, these were perceived as rather vague and failed to guide the students on what to look for in their peers' work.

With the wisdom of hindsight and after a critical analysis of the VE procedure, a modified approach has been designed. The main changes introduced in the redesigned version are: (1) the incorporation of synchronous partner sessions, including a synchronous peer feedback meeting, (2) reduction in the number of PA rounds, (3) formulating a new set of PA criteria, and (4) providing the students with more detailed guidance on using the criteria. The following paragraphs describe the modified version of the VE that is yet to be trialled. As it is a proposed model which can be further modified for other VE projects, the participant groups are referred to as ESP (English for Specific Purposes) groups and NS (Native-Speaker) students.

The modified VE project is designed for two months in total, with at least four synchronous sessions supplemented with asynchronous communication. As before, the final product, i.e. a tourist brochure, is prepared in pairs by students from the same institution and then further developed on the basis of the feedback received from their VE partners. The objective of the first introductory session, ideally conducted as a videoconference involving all ESP participants, is to offer the students an opportunity to get to know each other and learn about their respective study programmes and institutions. Alternatively, if arranging a group videoconference is not possible, the first meeting will be arranged individually by the students outside the regular class hours. The next two synchronous sessions between the ESP partners are used to discuss the typical aims, structure, and content of a tourist brochure, exchange ideas about the planning stage of the task, and offer each other initial peer feedback. The last synchronous session between the ESP groups is devoted to the first round of peer feedback. The second round of PA is provided by the NS students and sent to the original authors by email.

3. Assessment

It must be underlined here that the objective of the procedure described below is not to provide an overview of the whole VE and corresponding assessment processes, but to depict the steps necessary to familiarise the students with their roles in PA, who, in this particular context, have never experienced PA before (cf. Verzella & Sendur, 2019). Ideally, the same procedure should be implemented in both ESP course groups, as the students are engaged in the same task and offer one another peer feedback according to the same criteria. Due to differing course objectives, the set of assessment criteria used by the NS students may focus in greater detail on the language-related aspects, such as foreign language (L2) accuracy and the use of appropriate rhetorical strategies and persuasive discourse.

Step 1 – *Orientation*: in order to better orient instructional planning and the design of the VE project, during the first session, the teacher talks with the students about their prior writing instruction in the L2 classroom and their learning strategies related to this skill. Additionally, the students are asked about their experience of collaborative learning and using technology for general and learning purposes.

Step 2 – *Task setting*: the teacher introduces the task, i.e. collaborative work that aims at designing a tourist brochure for a specific target group, and explains the approach to writing adopted in this particular VE project. The students are informed that they are to plan, look for relevant information, and design a travel brochure advertising a tourist destination of their choice. They learn that they will have a chance to discuss these issues and exchange perspectives through synchronous and asynchronous communication tools with peers from another country enrolled in a similar ESP course. If necessary, the basic features (editing, saving, commenting, etc.) of Google Docs, the editing tool selected for the purposes of this project, are explained and practised.

Step 3 – *Analysis of a model text and introduction of assessment criteria*: on the basis of model examples, students discuss the characteristics of a tourist brochure. In particular, they focus on such aspects as the content strategy and structure, the relevance of the text to the target group, and the design and use of visual aids. As regards the language-related aspects, the students list vocabulary and grammar structures typical of such texts. The assessment criteria (see Table 1 below) are explained gradually by means of leading questions, e.g. how many parts does a travel brochure consist of? What is the objective of each part? What makes the brochure potentially appealing to the target group? As both groups are set exactly the same tasks, a common set of criteria is devised by the two instructors.

Step 4 – *Practising the use of assessment criteria*: the students in both ESP groups are presented the same/similar travel brochures (e.g. designed by students in previous years) and in small groups try to assess the text against the student assessment grid discussed earlier. Next, during the whole-class discussion, the students present their feedback and justify their choices. This creates space for exchanging ideas and practising the use of the criteria, and, at the same time, enables the teacher to intervene in cases of misunderstandings or biased judgement.

Table 1. A sample student assessment grid

Student assessment grid			
Criteria	1 Not at all	2 To some extent	3 Yes, fully
CONTENT STRATEGY AND STRUCTURE			
The material is ordered in a way that is logical, clear, and easy to follow.			
The text is divided into paragraphs.			
Precise and relevant headings are used.			
The content is relevant to the target group (international tourists aged 20-30).			
Comments:			
DESIGN AND USE OF VISUAL AIDS			
The layout (arrangement of text, graphics, colours) is well-designed and carefully prepared.			
There is a good balance of text and visual aids.			
The visual aids well illustrate the content.			
Comments:			
USE OF GRAMMAR AND LEXICAL ITEMS			
Lexical items: Tourism-related vocabulary is used (vocabulary listed during class discussions).			
Grammar: The target audience is addressed directly (e.g. second person pronouns, direct questions).			
Comments:			

Step 5 – *Preparation of the first draft and the first round of PA*: in pairs, the students from the same institution plan their work, research relevant information, and prepare the first draft of their brochures. During two synchronous online meetings, they have a chance to exchange ideas with their VE partners and ask for their opinion regarding the selected tourist attraction or illustrations. The real-time meetings are organised out of class at the times arranged by the students within the project time schedule. Once the first draft is ready, it is exchanged with the VE partners, who provide their feedback and justify their evaluations in the comment section of the grid. Additionally, the assessors are encouraged to leave more detailed comments/corrections in the Google Docs file. Then, the ESP groups meet during the final synchronous session to discuss their mutual evaluations and comments. This stage of PA is later briefly summarised in-class.

Step 6 – *Composing and sharing the second drafts with the NS project partners*: after the second draft is completed, it is sent to the NS partners, who offer their peer feedback on the basis of the common set of criteria created by the ESP instructors. The students should be encouraged to leave comments in the margins and tracked, in-text corrections in the document. Depending on the character of the NS class, additional criteria connected with the students' specialist expertise can be devised for these assessors. For instance, the NS participants of the original project were enrolled in a composition course; therefore, apart from the feedback on the design and the use of visual aids, which could be done by students of all kinds of specialisations, this group was additionally asked to comment on the content, structure, and rhetorical strategies. With NS partners, more emphasis can also be put on language-related aspects. Then the students return the corrected brochures by email to the original authors. In the final steps, the ESP students introduce the corrections and submit the final products to the teacher.

4. Conclusions and lessons learnt

Our experience shows us that learner autonomy should not be taken for granted in tertiary level students (e.g. Czura & Baran-Łucarz, 2021). At the beginning of the original project, students in the Polish institution voiced their concerns about the need to work collaboratively and provide feedback to each other. They admitted that they would rather receive more straightforward instructions from the teacher. Whereas the Italian students looked forward to receiving feedback from native speakers of English, they expressed their doubt about the quality of feedback offered by inexperienced students from the partner institution (Verzella & Sendur, 2019). Consequently, we were aware that PA needs to take a step-by-step approach and be adapted to students' needs and beliefs. Naturally, in other projects the level of scaffolding will depend on students' familiarity with this mode of assessment and their autonomous learning skills.

Although the same approaches to assessment in all partner institutions are on the whole not essential to the success of a VE project (Czura & Dooly, 2021), given the complexity of the current initiative that involved three partner institutions, each with a distinctive role, and several rounds of peer feedback, we think it is necessary to set the same assessment criteria for all the ESP participants. Clearly defined criteria and common standards will help the students prepare their brochures, provide more reliable feedback, and understand the corrective comments they will receive from their peers. As can be seen above, the assessment criteria were presented and discussed on the basis of a model text, which, in our view, helps students better conceptualise the criteria and adds to the authenticity of the task. We understand that sometimes, for various reasons, it is impossible for all participating institutions to agree on common assessment procedures and criteria. In a situation where the partners are assigned different tasks (like the NS group in the current project) or PA is carried out only within one partner institution, the compatibility of criteria is not essential and students can be encouraged to formulate assessment criteria themselves under the teacher's guidance.

In the modified VE procedure, we added synchronous PA sessions. It was motivated by the findings of the study conducted by Zheng, Cui, Li, and Huang (2018), according to which synchronous sessions between students engaged in PA provided a valuable forum for discussing the feedback and eliminating any misunderstandings. It was revealed that such synchronous meetings "significantly improved students' writing performance, qualitative feedback quality, meta-cognitive awareness, and self-efficacy" (Zheng et al., 2018, p. 1). Additionally, the exploration of seven different PA designs indicated that "chances of fulfilling all the feedback functions, and discussing all the feedback aspects, increase when both written and oral feedback are being provided" (Van den Berg, Admiraa, & Pilot, 2006, p. 34). Apart from these research-proven benefits, the synchronous sessions will provide the participants with the possibility to practise their speaking skills in meaningful, authentic conversations, and engage in intercultural dialogues with peers from other cultural backgrounds.

The VE described here is rather complex and involves three institutions, some of which have different tasks to complete. The redesigned model ought to be treated as one of the many possible ways in which PA can be conducted in VE. It can be further modified and adapted to the specific needs of potential partners, their varying curricula, and expected learning outcomes. Our teaching experience shows that PA has a potential for improving students' own learning, enhancing the understanding of assessment criteria (cf. Czura, 2016) and, in the case of VE, creating a platform for authentic communication across cultures.

Recommended readings

O'Malley, J. M., & Pierce, L. V. (1996). *Authentic assessment for English language learners: practical approaches for teachers*. Addison Wesley Publishing Company.

Topping, K. J. (2018). *Using peer assessment to inspire reflection and learning*. Routledge.

References

Black, P., Harrison, C., Lee, C., Marshall, B., & William, D. (2003). *Assessment for learning: putting it into practice*. Open University Press.

Brown, H. D., & Abeywickrama, P. (2019). *Language assessment: principles and classroom practices* (3rd ed.). Pearson Education.

Cheng, W., & Warren, M. (2005). Peer assessment of language proficiency. *Language Testing*, *22*(1), 93-121. https://doi.org/10.1191/0265532205lt298oa

Czura, A. (2016). Wpływ oceny koleżeńskiej na lęk przed pisaniem u studentów. *Teraźniejszość – Człowiek – Edukacja*, *19*(4), 97-114.

Czura A., & Baran-Łucarz M. (2021). "A stressful unknown" or "an oasis"?: undergraduate students' perceptions of assessment in an in-class and online English phonetics course. *Íkala, 26*(3), 623-641. https://doi.org/10.17533/udea.ikala.v26n3a09

Czura, A., & Dooly, M. (2021). Foreign language assessment in virtual exchange – The ASSESSnet project. *Collated Papers for the ALTE 7th International Conference* (pp. 137-140). ALTE.

Deakin-Crick, R., Sebba, J., Harlen, W., Guoxing, Y., & Lawson, H. (2005). Systematic review of research evidence of the impact on students of self- and peer-assessment. Protocol. In *Research Evidence in Education Library*. EPPI-Centre, Social Science Research Unit, Institute of Education, University of London.

Dooly, M. (2022). TEAMMATES in virtual exchange: tool and tips for peer assessment. In A. Czura & M. Dooly (Eds), *Assessing virtual exchange in foreign language courses at tertiary level* (pp. 107-120). Research-publishing.net. https://doi.org/10.14705/rpnet.2022.59.1413

Dooly, M., & Sadler, R. (2019). "If you don't improve, what's the point?" Investigating the impact of a "flipped" online exchange in teacher education. *ReCALL* FirstView, 1-21. https://doi.org/10.1017/S0958344019000107

Dudley-Evans, T., & St John, M. J. (1998). *Developments in ESP. A multi-disciplinary approach*. Cambridge University Press.

Ennis, M. J., Verzella, M., Montanari, S., Sendur, A. M., Simeonova Pissarro, M., Kaiser, S., & Wimhurst, A. (2021). A telecollaboration project on giving online peer feedback: implementing a multilateral virtual exchange during a pandemic. *Journal of Language and Education, 7*(4), 66-82. https://doi.org/10.17323/jle.2021.11914

Gielen, M., & De Wever, B. (2015). Structuring the peer assessment process: a multilevel approach for the impact on product improvement and peer feedback quality. *Journal of Computer Assisted Learning, 31*(5), 435-449. https://doi.org/10.1111/jcal.12096

Hattie, J., & Timperley, H. (2007). The power of feedback. *Review of Educational Research, 77*(1), 81-112. https://doi.org/10.3102/003465430298487

Little D., & Perclová R. (2001). *The European language portfolio: a guide for teachers and teacher trainers*. Council of Europe.

Peng, J. (2010). Peer assessment in an EFL context: attitudes and correlations. *Selected Proceedings of the 2008 Second Language Research Forum*. www.lingref.com/cpp/slrf/2008/paper2387.pdf

Sevilla-Pavón, A., & Haba-Osca, J. (2017). Learning from real-life and not books: a gamified approach to business English task design in transatlantic telecollaboration. *Iberica, 33*, 235-260.

Sluijsmans, D. M. A, Brand-Gruwel, S., & van Merriënboer, J. J. G. (2002). Peer assessment training in teacher education: effects on performance and perceptions. *Assessment & Evaluation in Higher Education, 27*(5), 443-454. https://doi.org/10.1080/0260293022000009311

Van de Kraak, S., & Lai, J. (2020). Virtual exchange strengthens international youth work. In F. Helm & A. Beaven (Eds), *Designing and implementing virtual exchange – a collection of case studies* (pp. 219-230). Research-publishing.net. https://doi.org/10.14705/rpnet.2020.45.1128

Van den Berg, I., Admiraa, W., & Pilot, A. (2006). Peer assessment in university teaching: evaluating seven course designs. *Assessment & Evaluation in Higher Education, 31*(1), 19-36. https://doi.org/10.1080/02602930500262346

Verzella, M., & Sendur, A. M. (2019). A telecollaboration project on writing for tourism: exploring thematic patterns in feedback exchanged by Italian, Polish, and Ukrainian students with US peer reviewers. In M. Ennis & G. Petri (Eds), *Teaching English for tourism. Bridging research and praxis.* (pp. 170-193). Routledge. https://doi.org/10.4324/9780429032141-8

Vinagre, M., & Muñoz, B. (2011). Computer-mediated corrective feedback and language accuracy in telecollaborative exchanges. *Language Learning & Technology, 15*(1), 72-103. https://doi.org/10125/44238

Vuylsteke, J.-F. (2022). Business communication skills through virtual exchange – a case study. In A. Czura & M. Dooly (Eds), A*ssessing virtual exchange in foreign language courses at tertiary level* (pp. 147-162). Research-publishing.net. https://doi.org/10.14705/rpnet.2022.59.1416

Ware, P., & Cañado, M. (2007). Chapter 6. Grammar and feedback: turning to language form in telecollaboration. In R. O'Dowd (Ed.), *Online intercultural exchange: an introduction for foreign language teachers* (pp. 107-126). Multilingual Matters. https://doi.org/10.21832/9781847690104-008

Ware, P. D., & O'Dowd, R. (2008). Peer feedback on language form in telecollaboration. *Language Learning & Technology, 12*(1), 43-63.

Zheng, L., Cui, P., Li, X., & Huang, R. (2018). Synchronous discussion between assessors and assessees in web-based peer assessment: impact on writing performance, feedback quality, meta-cognitive awareness and self-efficacy. *Assessment and Evaluation in Higher Education, 43*(3), 500-514. https://doi.org/10.1080/02602938.2017.1370533

7. TEAMMATES in virtual exchange: tool and tips for peer assessment

Melinda Dooly[1]

Abstract

Virtual Exchange (VE) in higher education often involves small, online working groups who meet outside of class time. This lack of teacher presence in the meetings has its advantages (e.g. more student-centred, more autonomous environments); however, it also presents challenges for assessment. This chapter introduces an online platform called TEAMMATES and briefly describes how it has been used for continuous peer assessment in an ongoing VE between two university classes in language teacher education.

Keywords: peer assessment, virtual exchange, telecollaboration contract, digital communicative competences.

1. Introduction

As the use of communication technology for connecting learners has grown exponentially in language teaching, there has been a movement to consolidate the pedagogical foundations for VE (see Dooly & Vinagre, 2021 for an historical overview of other terms applied). As is evident in many of the chapters in this book, the origins of VE have long been attributed to the influence of the Communicative Approach (CA) in language teaching (Brammerts, 1996; Dooly, 2010, 2017; Kern, 1996; Kurek & Müller-Hartmann, 2017; Vinagre, 2016). It is important to underscore its impact on language teaching,

---

1. Universitat Autònoma de Barcelona, Spain; melindaann.dooly@uab.cat; https://orcid.org/0000-0002-1478-4892

How to cite: Dooly, M. (2022). TEAMMATES in virtual exchange: tool and tips for peer assessment. In A. Czura & M. Dooly (Eds), *Assessing virtual exchange in foreign language courses at tertiary level* (pp. 107-120). Research-publishing.net. https://doi.org/10.14705/rpnet.2022.59.1413

learning, and assessment, and subsequently VE. In particular, CA has a role in understanding learning objectives and how to assess these goals "in terms of *language use*" (Thornbury, 2013, p. 188; this author's emphasis). In this sense, the VE pedagogical design is often based on CA principles (Dooly & Vinagre, 2021). Teachers feel VE can best encompass the use of meaningful tasks that create opportunities for spontaneous use of the target language for genuine communication. However, assessment presents a challenge for pedagogical application of VE and, as Hauck, Müller-Hartmann, Rienties, and Rogaten (2020) point out, the assessment process (inevitably should) tie back to the task design for the VE.

This chapter describes the peer assessment used during a VE in language teacher education in which the telecollaborative activities, as part of the course design, form a central nexus for the learning process (Fuchs, 2021). A principal aim of the course is to foment the active engagement of future language teachers in communicative online situations that facilitates learning (content and language). The aim is that they can experience and reflect on how to transfer this knowledge to similar contexts for their pupils, departing from the baseline of CA in language education. The two teacher educators plan the course programme together (despite being listed in their relevant university programmes as different subjects) so that both groups are expected to do the same principal activities and go through a similar evaluation process, including peer evaluation across international borders.

This chapter describes the use of an online platform for peer assessment that can be easily integrated into the VE pedagogical design in language teacher and Foreign Language (FL) education. The VE in question began in 2003 and has been ongoing ever since (see Dooly & Sadler, 2016, 2020, for more details of the evolution and current state of the VE). What is of interest to this chapter are the weekly online meetings carried out in small work groups, held outside of class, and during the entire course. Together the working groups design a telecollaborative language learning project and their collaboration is one of the components of the VE that is assessed through the platform TEAMMATES (explained in more detail below). Moreover, because the student teachers are learning about CA and language teaching, the tool is combined with descriptors aligned with the Common European Framework of Reference for languages (CEFR; Council of Europe, 2020).

The principal theoretical underpinnings of the teaching approach of this course lie in the seminal work done by Vygotsky (1986), which highlights the role of mediated action (and interaction) as central to the learning process as well as placing particular emphasis on student-centred learning (Bruner, 1961; Schulman, 1986; von Glaserfeld, 1989; see also Dooly, 2022, this volume, for discussion of the 'student-centredness' of VE). The design of the VE aims to ensure that the online meetings, integrated into the overall teaching programme lead "to (a) uptake of ideas, (b) scaffolding to ensure conceptual understanding, and (c) handover – that is, successful transfer and assimilation of new knowledge into already existing knowledge and understanding" (Dooly & Sadler, 2020, p. 6). Inevitably, this handover of knowledge entails a significant amount of learner autonomy, in particular in VE settings (Cappellini, Lewis, & Rivens Mompean, 2017; Fuchs, 2021; Marjanovic, Dooly, & Sadler, 2021). Peer evaluation has been put forth as a relevant means of promoting learner autonomy (Little & Perclová, 2001), although this must be supported and facilitated through instruction, training, and empirical learning of peer evaluation procedures (Czura & Sendur, 2022, this volume).

Peer assessment has been touted as a means to provide learners with key opportunities to take responsibility for their learning, including critical reflection (analysis), monitoring and applying critical evaluation of theirs and their peers' outcomes as well as the learning process (Chew, Snee, & Price, 2016; Topping, 1998) although many scholars suggest that for learners who are not fully autonomous, teacher support in providing feedback is more effective (Lantolf & Poehner, 2008; Lyster & Ranta, 1997; Sauro, 2009).

Thus, peer evaluation (of both in-class and VE activities) is continuously present throughout the course. These evaluations were included in our pedagogical design to support the students' growing awareness of the need to be responsible for their own learning, which has been advocated as a key foundation for effective telecollaboration (O'Rourke, 2007; Ushioda, 2000; Warschauer & Kern, 2000) as well as promoting student-centred learning through technology (Thomas, Reinder, & Warschauer, 2013). However, the efficacy and success of CA approaches such as VE does not lie only in the technical teacher know-how; innovation in the underlying pedagogy is also germane. One of the key aspects of teacher competences in VE environments is the promotion of learner autonomy (Dooly, 2010; O'Rourke, 2007; The EVALUATE Group, 2019); thus as future teachers, experiencing and practising peer evaluation during VE can provide a basis for empirical development of this key teacher competence.

2. Overview of the VE project

TEAMMATES[2] was first used as a tool for peer assessment by the author during her long-term collaboration with another teacher based in the USA (at the University of Illinois Urbana Champaign). The collaboration between our courses began in 2003 after 'meeting online' through a mutual contact and has continued, non-stop, since 2004 (Dooly & Sadler, 2016, 2020; Sadler & Dooly, 2013). The students are studying to become language teachers; most of them will teach English as L2 or as an FL, others will teach other languages. The language they will teach depends on the student profile of that year because both courses (in Spain and in the USA) have a percentage of international students who will return to their countries and teach their languages as L2.

The course covers various aspects of technology-infused language teaching. Three main areas that are covered are (1) theories of language acquisition; (2) the design of FL (or L2) teaching activities within project-based language learning approaches, including VE; and (3) the integration of technologies in learning FLs (methods, planning, effective application of resources, etc.). Because the students are studying VE as an approach, their own VE experience is considered to be vital to their professional development. This implies that

---

2. https://teammatesv4.appspot.com/web/front/home

their participation in the VE should be taken into consideration as part of their final evaluation at the end of the course. Discussion of the importance of active participation (which goes beyond simply 'being there') is carried out at the beginning of the course and the students are given a 'telecollaboration contract' (see supplementary materials Appendix 1) so they are aware of the descriptors that are used for evaluation.

As future language teachers, the expected learning outcomes of the students covers several domains: academic competences such as being able to develop criteria and materials for embedding technology and VE into teacher practice; linguistic competences such as being able to communicate effectively in tasks related to teaching in both in-person and online sessions; and professional competences that include working effectively in collaboration with others both in-class and telecollaboratively.

TEAMMATES is not used to evaluate all of the above competences since the students are engaged in many more activities than only the VE. TEAMMATES is used for the evaluation of their online collaboration as well as providing insight into their preparation prior to taking part in activities (the VE is considered to be the institutional tasks even though they take place outside of class hours).

3. Assessment

TEAMMATES was developed in 2010 and we began to use the platform in 2013. For the moment, the platform is free for use although it is stipulated in the webpage that the company will "provide its services free for as long as [they] can". The platform was designed by teachers and learners for use by members of the educational community. Students can provide peer evaluations through any device that has an internet connection and are not required to have an account to access the evaluations; however, students with a TEAMMATES account will be able to see the entire record of their peer evaluations. Students without an account can only access the current peer evaluation and are responsible for storing their evaluations as a PDF if they wish to keep a record.

Teachers must have an account to create the evaluation templates for their students. The dashboard of the programme is not overly 'user friendly' and requires some time to become acquainted with all its functions; however, once an evaluation template has been set and used, it becomes easier. It is recommended to do a few test runs before applying the system to an actual class setting.

A key feature that has proven worthwhile for our VE is the possibility to set up pre-established groups for 'team peer evaluation sessions'. The assessment between teams can be set as anonymous for their peers while the teachers can see the overall evaluations as well as receive confidential observations from the different members of the teams. This allows the teachers to intervene in a timely fashion in the event that the team cohesion or collaboration appears to be unsatisfactory.

The assessments can be (pre)scheduled to be opened, then closed and available to each team member at specific intervals, which ensures feedback after all the meetings (or randomly if preferred) and it is not necessary for the teacher to remember to do so after each meeting (see Figure "Setting up scheduling of TEAMMATES surveys" in supplementary materials). This is especially useful if the groups have meetings scheduled at different timetables.

The evaluations can be set so that group members not only receive feedback from other team members, but there can also be feedback between teams – a useful feature for activities that include demonstrating and discussing output between smaller groups in the VE classes. Students or teams can also receive individualised feedback from teachers, including invited lecturers. This makes the platform highly suitable for VE assessment which involves at least two, sometimes more partner teachers (see Figure "Grouping recipients for individualised feedback in TEAMMATES" in supplementary materials).

To keep the feedback brief but efficient (Figure 1), we try to keep the questions short and quick to answer, typically asking Likert scale questions for each team member and limiting the number of 'essay' type questions to optional (asking for a more reasoned reflection on their peers' performance) .

Figure 1. Simple-to-answer questions

> **Question 2:** How much did you learn from this individual about the materials (learning style) they were responsible for bringing to the meeting?
>
> Only the following persons can see your responses:
> - The receiving student can see your response, the name of the recipient, but not your name
> - Instructors in this course can see your response, the name of the recipient, and your name
>
> **Evaluee/Recipient**
>
> ▄▄▄▄▄▄▄▄▄▄▄▄▄ (Student)
> ○ I learned about it in depth and and was pushed to reflect.
> ○ I learned about it in depth
> ○ I learned but needed more depth
> ○ A little bit
> ○ Nothing
>
> 💬 [Optional] Comment on your response

Given the profile of our students (future language teachers), we focus some of our questions on collaborative partnership and leadership qualities (see Table 1). The descriptors we have elaborated are adapted from the domain of 'mediation' found in the CEFR (Council of Europe, 2020).

Table 1. Example of descriptors for leadership qualities

How well did your peer (NAME) take a lead role to organise communicative activity during the meeting? Choose one descriptor that best fits your peer's performance during this meeting.
S/he recognises undercurrents in interaction and takes appropriate steps accordingly to guide the direction of the talk. S/he almost always effectively leads the development of complex abstract topics, while guiding the discussion through key questions and encouragement to others to elaborate their ideas further.
S/he usually organises and manages collaborative group work efficiently. S/he gives precise instructions for group work and formulates questions and feedback to encourage mates to contribute to the ongoing assigned activities.
S/he sometimes builds on the other mates' ideas and links them into coherent lines of thinking. S/he occasionally explains how another idea (not necessarily own) fits with the main topic under discussion.
S/he does not intervene much and when does so, it is usually to provide informative sentences about their own ideas. S/he does little to encourage others to contribute to the discussion.

Chapter 7

We also ask for peer feedback on communicative competences in the language of instruction and communication between partners (English). Using TEAMMATES to do so provides us insight into communicative competences in online meetings that we do not normally have direct access to evaluating ourselves in face-to-face classes. Again, using the CEFR (Council of Europe, 2020) as a baseline for our questions, we might ask the group members to rank their peers according to descriptions as follows (Table 2).

Table 2. Example of descriptors for communicative skills in online meeting

How well did your peer (NAME) communicate during the meeting? Choose one descriptor that best fits your peer's performance during this meeting.
S/he communicates confidently and effectively for both professional (e.g. discussion of tasks, course content) and personal purposes (small talk, etc.). S/he is able to adapt and even support other speakers, even those with thicker accents or is evidently struggling with the target language.
S/he communicates effectively for both professional (e.g. discussion of tasks, course content) and personal purposes (small talk, etc.). S/he has some problems understanding others with thicker accents or problems using the target language but quickly asks for clarification.
S/he communicates through relatively simple language use for professional (e.g. discussion of tasks, course content). Does not participate much in personal discussions (small talk, etc.). Does not typically engage with others with thicker accents or with apparent difficulties in the target language.
Hardly interacts with others and when does so, uses short, extremely simple utterances.

Many proponents of VE have argued that these learning environments are ideal for promoting the digital skills required in modern society (Bates, 2011; Dooly, 2017; The EVALUATE Group, 2019). Given that the recent adaptations to the CEFR now include digital interactions, we have also adapted these descriptors for the peer assessments in TEAMMATES for our VE (see Table 3).

Table 3. Example of descriptors for digital communicative skills in online meeting

How well did your peer (NAME) perform digitally during the meeting? Choose one descriptor that best fits your peer's performance during this meeting.
S/he can express their ideas with clarity and precision. Regularly combines audio, text and available technology for highly effective communication (e.g. screensharing, camera position, etc.).

S/he can express their ideas with clarity and precision. Sometimes combines audio, text and available technology for effective communication (e.g. screensharing, camera position, etc.).
S/he can express their ideas with some help. Infrequently combines audio, text and available technology but efforts do not always result in effective communication (e.g. screensharing, camera position, etc.).
Hardly interacts with others orally, prefers text only. Positioning with the camera seems awkward at times.

4. Conclusions and lessons learnt

It is important to underscore that the first evaluations and exchanges often create student anxiety as they are not always familiar with the concept of interdependence in the learning process and activities which can promote it (Chew et al., 2016; Czura & Sendur, 2022, this volume; Dooly & Sadler, 2020; Panadero, Romero, & Strijbos, 2013). Some adaptation, support, and open dialogue is necessary to move students towards more autonomous learning and an acceptance of continuous peer evaluations. The challenges and pushback from students regarding peer assessment have been well documented elsewhere (Alfares, 2017; Czura & Sendur, 2022, this volume; Forrester & Tashchian, 2010; Jacobs & Loh, 2003). For instance, during one iteration of our VE, a student received quite negative peer feedback reports at the beginning of the exchange. In a private email to the teacher following the report, the student was angry and concerned about the report, expressing that she felt it was 'unfair' and she was uncomfortable being judged by her peers. Nonetheless, she soon followed peer suggestions and became notably more participative, both in-class and online. This was subsequently reflected in higher peer evaluations of her performance. She also began to take more initiative as a group leader and became a 'champion' of peer feedback as an effective teaching strategy (see Dooly & Sadler, 2020 for a more detailed account).

A key strategy we have found to be most effective for dealing with student anxiety regarding peer assessment is to always schedule time for discussion about the process during in-person classes. At the beginning, dialogue is best focused on the purpose of the continuous assessment. We include a 'telecollaboration contract' (see supplementary materials Appendix 1) which is a type of voluntary 'learning contract' that outlines key behaviours and actions for successful VEs. This contract is signed by the student as a pledge to engage in specific, positive collaborative learning behaviours. Students are assured that the contract goes three ways: the group can lodge 'breach of contract' complaints against other mates and even the teachers. It is important to note, however, that we insist that detailed accounts of steps taken to improve telecollaborative relations between the group members must be provided before a group is allowed to claim breach of contract and before moving to 'fire' a group member. The contract also serves as an outline of the criteria that will be used for the peer assessment through TEAMMATES and as factors to be taken into account at the end of the exchange when students are required to submit longer, informed reports of their group activities and performance.

There must also be time and space for dialogue during the exchange to deal with students' feelings of anxiety and potential resentment for having to and being continuously 'judged' by their peers. Learners are not necessarily comfortable with these roles (Panadero et al., 2013) and students may feel that this should solely be the teachers' responsibility (Strijbos et al., 2009). Referencing the telecollaboration contract and the importance that learner autonomy has for language learning are valuable points for supporting students' acceptance of the process, but the teacher must not forget that it is a gradual process that requires patience and understanding.

Data that has been analysed from different iterations of the VE described above have shown that the students gradually take on more and more responsibility for their learning (Dooly & Sadler, 2020). Despite evidence of some resistance to the pressures of continual peer assessment during the VE, the learners do begin to self-manage and monitor their own learning activities. The combination of peer learning and peer assessment promotes the interaction necessary for L2 learning, it also promotes learner responsibility and reflection. These processes can be facilitated through online platforms such as TEAMMATES so that the VE teachers can focus more on supporting the ongoing development of their pupils.

5. Supplementary materials

https://research-publishing.box.com/s/h07c4tblgshw86y0pwkkxvivvfzxgo3q

Recommended readings

Dooly, M., & Sadler, R. (2020). "If you don't improve, what's the point?" Investigating the impact of a "flipped" online exchange in teacher education. *ReCALL, 32*(1), 4-24. https://doi.org/10.1017/S0958344019000107

European Commission. (2020). *The digital education action plan (21-27)*. https://ec.europa.eu/education/sites/default/files/document-library-docs/deap-communication-sept2020_en.pdf

Hauck, M., & Müller-Hartmann, A. (2020). (Eds). *Virtual exchange and 21st century teacher education: short papers from the 2019 EVALUATE conference*. Research-publishing.net. https://doi.org/10.14705/rpnet.2020.46.9782490057801

References

Alfares, N. (2017). Benefits and difficulties of learning in group work in EFL classes in Saudi Arabia. *English Language Teaching, 10*(7), 247-256. https://doi.org/10.5539/elt.v10n7p247

Bates, T. (2011). Understanding web 2.0 and its implications for e-learning. In M. J. W. Lee & C. McLoughlin (Eds), *Web 2.0-based e-learning: applying social informatics for tertiary teaching* (pp. 21-42). IGI Global. https://doi.org/10.4018/978-1-60566-294-7.ch002

Brammerts, H. (1996). Language learning in tandem using the internet. In M. Warschauer (Ed.), *Telecollaboration in foreign language learning* (pp. 121-130). University of Hawai'i Press.

Bruner, J. S. (1961). The act of discovery. *Harvard Educational Review, 31*(1), 21-32.

Cappellini, M., Lewis, T., & Rivens Mompean, A. (2017). (Eds). *Learner autonomy and web 2.0*. Equinox Publishing.

Chew, E., Snee, H., & Price, T. (2016). Enhancing international postgraduates' learning experience with online peer assessment and feedback innovation. *Innovations in Education and Teaching International, 53*(3), 247-259. https://doi.org/10.1080/14703297.2014.937729

Council of Europe. (2020). *Common European framework of reference for languages: learning, teaching, assessment – companion volume*. Council of Europe Publishing. www.coe.int/lang-cefr.

Czura, A., & Sendur, A. M. (2022). Peer assessment of process writing in a virtual exchange project. In A. Czura & M. Dooly (Eds), *Assessing virtual exchange in foreign language courses at tertiary level* (pp. 93-106). Research-publishing.net. https://doi.org/10.14705/rpnet.2022.59.1412

Dooly, M. (2010). The teacher 2.0. In S. Guth & F. Helm (Eds), *Telecollaboration 2.0. language, literacies and intercultural learning in the 21st century* (pp. 277-303). Peter Lang.

Dooly, M. (2017). Telecollaboration. In C. Chapelle & S. Sauro (Eds), *The handbook of technology in second language teaching and learning* (pp. 169-183). Wiley-Blackwell. https://doi.org/10.1002/9781118914069.ch12

Dooly, M. (2022). The evolution of virtual exchange and assessment practices. In A. Czura & M. Dooly (Eds), *Assessing virtual exchange in foreign language courses at tertiary level* (pp. 13-27). Research-publishing.net. https://doi.org/10.14705/rpnet.2022.59.1407

Dooly, M., & Sadler, R. (2016). Becoming little scientists: technologically-enhanced project-based language learning. *Technology & Language Learning, 20*(1), 54-78. https://doi.org/10125/44446

Dooly, M., & Sadler, R. (2020). "If you don't improve, what's the point?" Investigating the impact of a "flipped" online exchange in teacher education. *ReCALL, 32*(1), 4-24. https://doi.org/10.1017/S0958344019000107

Dooly, M., & Vinagre, M. (2021). Research into practice: virtual exchange in language teaching and learning. *Language Teaching*, 1-15. https://doi.org/10.1017/S0261444821000069

Forrester, W. R., & Tashchian, A. (2010). Effects of personality on attitudes toward academic group work. *American Journal of Business Education, 3*(3), 39-46. https://doi.org/10.19030/ajbe.v3i3.397

Fuchs, C. (2021). Supporting autonomy in an exam-based context: results from a Hong Kong-US telecollaboration. In C. Fuchs, M. Hauck & M. Dooly (Eds), *Language education in digital spaces: perspectives on autonomy and interaction* (pp. 61-84). Springer. https://doi.org/10.1007/978-3-030-74958-3_4

Hauck, M., Müller-Hartmann, A., Rienties, B., & Rogaten, J. (2020). Approaches to researching digital-pedagogical competence development in VE-based teacher education. *Journal of Virtual Exchange, 3*(SI), 5-35. https://doi.org/10.21827/jve.3.36082

Jacobs, G. M., & Loh, W. I. (2003). Using cooperative learning in large classes. In M. Cherian & R. Mau (Eds), *Large classes* (pp. 142-157). McGraw-Hill.

Kern, R. (1996). Computer-mediated communication: using e-mail exchanges to explore personal histories in two cultures. In M. Warschauer (Ed.), *Telecollaboration in foreign language learning* (pp. 105-120). University of Hawai'i Press.

Kurek, M., & Müller-Hartmann, A. (2017). Task design for telecollaborative exchanges: in search of new criteria. *System, 64*, 7-20. https://doi.org/10.1016/j.system.2016.12.004

Lantolf, J. P., & Poehner, M. E. (2008). Dynamic assessment. In N. H. Hornberger (Ed.), *Encyclopedia of language and education 2nd edition, Volume 7: language testing and assessment* (pp. 273-284). Springer.

Little D., & Perclová R. (2001). *The European language portfolio: a guide for teachers and teacher trainers*. Council of Europe.

Lyster, R., & Ranta, L. (1997). Corrective feedback and learner uptake: negotiation of form in communicative classrooms. *Studies in Second Language Acquisition, 19*(1), 37-66. https://doi.org/10.1017/S0272263197001034

Marjanovic, J., Dooly, M., & Sadler, R. (2021). From autonomous learners to self-directed teachers in telecollaboration: teachers look back and reflect. In C. Fuchs, M. Hauck & M. Dooly (Eds), *Language education in digital spaces: perspectives on autonomy and interaction* (pp. 113-133). Springer. https://doi.org/10.1007/978-3-030-74958-3_6

O'Rourke, B. (2007). Models of telecollaboration (1): eTandem. In R. O'Dowd (Ed.), *Online intercultural exchange: an introduction to foreign language teachers* (pp. 41-61). Multilingual Matters. https://doi.org/10.21832/9781847690104-005

Panadero, E., Romero, M., & Strijbos, J. W. (2013). The impact of a rubric and friendship on construct validity of peer assessment, perceived fairness and comfort, and performance. *Studies In Educational Evaluation, 39*(4), 195-203. https://doi.org/10.1016/j.stueduc.2013.10.005

Sadler, R., & Dooly, M. (2013). Filling in the gaps: linking theory and practice through telecollaboration in teacher education. *ReCALL, 25*(1), 4-29. https://doi.org/10.1017/S0958344012000237

Sauro, S. (2009). Computer-mediated corrective feedback and the development of L2 Grammar. *Language Learning and Technology, 13*, 96-120. http://llt.msu.edu/vol13num1/sauro.pdf

Schulman, L. S. (1986). Those who understand: knowledge growth and teaching. *Educational Researcher, 15*(2), 4-14. https://doi.org/10.3102/0013189X015002004

Strijbos, J. W., Ochoa, T. A., Sluijsmans, D. M. A., Segers, M. S. R., & Tillema, H. H. (2009). Fostering interactivity through formative peer assessment in (web-based) collaborative learning environments. In C. Mourlas, N. Tsianos & P. Germanakos (Eds), *Cognitive and emotional processes in web-based education: integrating human factors and personalization* (pp. 375-395). IGI Global. https://doi.org/10.4018/978-1-60566-392-0.ch018

The EVALUATE Group. (2019). *Evaluating the impact of virtual exchange on initial teacher education: a European policy experiment*. Research-publishing.net. https://doi.org/10.14705/rpnet.2019.29.9782490057337

Thomas, M., Reinder, H., & Warschauer, M. (2013). Contemporary computer-assisted language learning: the role of digital media and incremental change. In M. Thomas, H. Reinder & M. Warschauer (Eds), *Contemporary computer-assisted language learning* (pp. 1-12). Bloomsbury.

Thornbury, S. (2013). Language teaching methodology. In J. Simpson (Ed.), *The Routledge handbook of applied linguistics* (pp. 185-199). Routledge.

Topping, K. J. (1998). Peer assessment between students in colleges and universities. *Review of Educational Research, 68*(3), 249-276. https://doi.org/10.3102/00346543068003249

Ushioda, E. (2000). Tandem language learning via e-mail: from motivation to autonomy. *ReCALL, 12*(2), 21-28. https://doi.org/10.1017/s0958344000000124

Vinagre, M. (2016). Developing key competences for life-long learning through virtual collaboration: teaching ICT in English as a medium of instruction. In C. Wang & L. Winstead (Eds), *Handbook of research on foreign language education in the digital age* (pp. 170-187). IGI Global. https://doi.org/10.4018/978-1-5225-0177-0.ch008

Von Glaserfeld, E. (1989). Constructivism in education. In T. Husèn & N. Postlewaite (Eds), *International encyclopedia of education* (pp. 162-163). Pergamon Press.

Vygotsky, L. S. (1986). *Thought and language*. MIT Press.

Warschauer, M., & Kern, R. (2000). *Network-based language teaching: concepts and practice*. Cambridge University Press. https://doi.org/10.1017/CBO9781139524735

Part 3.

Case studies at tertiary level

8 Is (inter)cultural competence accessible? Assessing for fluency

Grace Dolcini[1] and Grit Matthias Phelps[2]

Abstract

Globalization and the digitalization of our lives have made it impossible to avoid (inter)cultural encounters. In the traditional classroom environment, students are expected to juggle a myriad of choices almost simultaneously. Factors like grammar, pronunciation, word choice, etc. are all important assessment factors to consider when looking at the accuracy of the students' target language performance. However this changes considerably in Virtual Exchange (VE) courses with a primary goal of fluency. In this case, the assessment should take into account social cues, silence, turn taking, correction, reactions to new ideas, signal words, and speaker confidence, among others. In this article, we would like to share our ideas of how we assess a fluency course using a modified version of Byram's (1997) model for teaching and assessing intercultural communicative competence and provide an example of a course design that was particularly successful, in which students worked together to complete a poster about the 100-year anniversary of the Bauhaus School. Additionally, to create an environment that promotes learner autonomy and helps students fully experience empathy, understanding, and tolerance while collaborating, a portfolio of tasks and self-assessment journals were used.

Keywords: assessment, collaboration, fluency, intercultural competence, virtual exchange.

---

1. Bielefeld Universität, Bielefeld, Germany; grace.dolcini@uni-bielefeld.de

2. Cornell University, Ithaca, New York, United States; gritmatthias@cornell.edu

How to cite: Dolcini, G., & Matthias Phelps, G. (2022). Is (inter)cultural competence accessible? Assessing for fluency. In A. Czura & M. Dooly (Eds), *Assessing virtual exchange in foreign language courses at tertiary level* (pp. 123-134). Research-publishing.net. https://doi.org/10.14705/rpnet.2022.59.1414

Chapter 8

1. Introduction

Globalization and the digitalization of our lives have made it impossible to avoid intercultural communication. Encounters with foreign cultures are not limited to holiday trips over the summer break. Workplaces, schools, and neighborhoods in the USA and Europe (and around the rest of the world) have developed into communities whose many members have a different cultural identity and/or come from families with mixed national, ethnic, and religious backgrounds. It is imperative then that Foreign Language (FL) courses prepare students to interact appropriately with speakers from other countries in different communicative contexts.

The definition for what 'appropriately' could mean in this context has a few possibilities. The approach adopted for the purposes of our project complies with the standards set by the American Council on the Teaching of Foreign Languages (ACTFL, 2006), which underline the ability to converse with openness and also the willingness to put themselves in the place of the other speaker. Consequently, mutual understanding, empathy, and curiosity are important components of FL education. In order to successfully incorporate these standards into our VE project, we have adapted the four axes described by Neuner (1994). The first axis is to become aware of one's own identity and (re)activate one's own cultural concept. The second axis refers to the ability to realize that everyone has a unique culturally determined understanding of the world. The third is empathy and underscores the need to understand cultural perspective of others: "From being ethnocentric and aware only of cultural phenomena as seen from their existing viewpoint, learners are to acquire an intercultural awareness which recognizes that such phenomena can be seen from a different perspective, from within a different culture and ethnic identity" (Byram, 1991, p. 19). As Kramsch (2011) underlines, "the challenge is to understand how and to what extent our perspective is culturally determined" (p. 365). Finally, the fourth axis, which is particularly important in the practice of VE, embraces tolerance to ambiguity, i.e. the ability to withstand difficult situations, especially when they cause strong emotional reactions. For instance, when the communicators' emotions might almost take over their actions, they need to be able to step back, examine the reasons and try to understand their interlocutors' motivations. This can only be applied and acquired solely through practice. With the hope of bringing a slice of the 'real world' into our classrooms, we implemented a VE during which our students could interact with peers from the target country. This created opportunities to practice authentic communication skills, tolerance of ambiguity, and intercultural competence in a safe and guided environment.

In the traditional classroom setting, students are expected to juggle a myriad of choices almost simultaneously. Factors such as grammar, pronunciation, or word choice are all important assessment factors to consider when looking at the accuracy of the students' target language performance. However, this changes considerably in VE courses, where fluency becomes the primary goal. In this case, the assessment should additionally take into account social cues, silence, turn taking, reactions to new ideas, signal words, and speaker confidence, among others. A student of both culture and language is competent at not just communicating in an FL, but also understanding how their speaking partners' perspectives might be shaped by their culture and personal experience (Byram, 1997).

So how do we assess these less-tangible factors? Many of FL textbooks used in language courses include information and exercises that introduce the learner to cultural specifics tied to language accuracy. Then, assessment in VE needs to address the following questions and focus on students' communicative skills.

- How do I tell my partner I disagree without sounding insulting?
- When and how do I interrupt my partner?
- What does it mean when my partner is silent?
- How would I feel about a positive or negative reaction to something I have said?
- How has my upbringing and background affected the way I view the world?

This shift from accuracy-oriented to communication-centered assessment is vitally important in a VE class and is symptomatic of a transition to new pedagogy: "By virtue of engaging learners in a dynamic process of inquiry, discovery, exploration, and interpretation, together with learners from another culture, such a project invariably favors a collective, constructivist approach to learning" (Furstenberg, 2010, p. 56). The constructivist approach assumes that students find culturally substantial meaning in the language they are studying. Instead of a language being reduced to just grammar and vocabulary, it suddenly becomes a means of communication between individuals that will also enable them to become global citizens and bring them a step closer to cultural competence.

In order to assess these intangible markers and solve this assessment conundrum, our universities have been experimenting together with different VE modules. Since our course is designed for fluency and not accuracy, the criteria for assessment focus on the participants' abilities to develop a sense of awareness, an openness and discovery of new ideas and viewpoints, and finally through all this, the confidence needed to communicate in a variety of situations. In this chapter, we would like to describe our approach to assessing a fluency course using a modified version of Byram's (1997) model for teaching and assessing intercultural communicative competence and provide an example of a course design that was particularly successful.

2. Overview of the VE project

In 2011, Grace Dolcini from the Fachsprachenzentrum (FL Center) at Bielefeld Universität and Grit Matthias Phelps from the German Department at Cornell University in Ithaca, New York, came together to create an online VE in which university students from diverse backgrounds could not only practice their fluency skills, but also connect with other participants living in another country. Student participants must have a minimum of B1 in the target language and C1 in the home university/native language (it should be noted that not all participants are native speakers – at both universities there are international students with a high competency level in the home institution language). All are assigned partners to meet twice a week for 50 minutes using synchronous computer mediated communication over the course of seven weeks. They remain with the same partner(s) for the duration of the project. During the exchange sessions students use solely English for half the time and solely German for the other half while discussing assigned topics and collaborative projects. These topics in most cases revolve around a central theme, which the entire course is based on, as well as the final project or a portfolio.

One of the challenges when designing this course is that both partner universities have different requirements. The students on the Bielefeld side take this course to either fulfill an elective requirement or to use it toward their internationalization module. For both of these cases, the entire course is contained in these seven weeks. However, on the Cornell side, the students are at the end of a semester-long course, and the VE is only one component of the requirements in the course. This is also challenging in terms of assessment since both universities have different policies on what is required of the students to successfully pass or receive a grade, as well as on how many credit points are awarded after course completion.

Despite these setbacks, our intention was never to create a tandem course with rigid guidelines and a strong focus on language correction and assessment. Although students have an opportunity to be corrected by their partners on lexical choices and grammar, the course does not base assessment on accuracy. In fact, no conversations are recorded for feedback, and the students work without teachers' direct supervision in their VE rooms to promote autonomy in their collaborative learning process. Instead, the objectives for the students are to boost their confidence in the ability to communicate their thoughts and opinions, to heighten their awareness of new ideas and viewpoints (especially in a collaborative context), and to practice their skills of negotiating non-verbal communication.

An important component to the course is that students are handed the responsibility for their learning outcomes. Although each meeting has a specific set of tasks within a theme, the partners themselves decide in what order to do the tasks, in what direction to take the conversation, and when to switch between the languages. They are also responsible for scheduling potential changes as well as any extra make-up or planning sessions for the final collaborative project. In addition, the tasks are designed to leave enough time for the partners to engage personally in topics of their choosing. In authentic communication, students will need to be able to comfortably and confidently negotiate their decisions and circumstances, and we believe these VE sessions are an important starting point.

Over the years, we have tried many different ideas with different results, but the main focus for both small and large tasks in our courses is an opportunity to collaborate and experience success. This is especially important in terms of creating scenarios where students can practice tolerance and learn to overcome conflict that may arise in difficult situations. Regardless of whether that means collaborating to gather information or to create an end product (like a poster or a video), all tasks are designed in a way that forces the students into situations in which they need to make decisions together and negotiate (with the correct meta language) what they want their collective outcome to be.

One particular semester, the course was designed around the 100-year anniversary of the Bauhaus School, and the students were assigned a set of tasks exploring the topic, its history, and influence around the world. The end assessment consisted in designing a poster for a contest (see supplementary materials Appendix 1 and Appendix 2 for syllabus plans in both institutions). These tasks mostly involved getting acquainted with readings and videos on different aspects of the theme and discussing these with VE partners. The students were also asked to reflect on the conversations in a journal on an ongoing basis.

A particularly interesting aspect for this semester was the fact that the final project created an opportunity for the students to have their work shown in a public setting. The main office of the Department of German Studies at Cornell needed new wall decoration, and it was decided that the Bielefeld group would vote on the project posters from their Cornell partners and determine which two posters would be hung in the office for the next few years (see supplementary materials Appendix 3). In addition, an exhibition which would include posters from both universities was planned at the beginning of the following semester in the lounge of the FL Center at Bielefeld University.

3. Assessment in the VE project

One of the prime benefits of exchanging with other language learners from another country is the experience of communicating with a person living in a different context. However, this adds a large list of extra factors that FL speakers must negotiate when formulating utterances in the target language. For the instructor, the question then becomes how and what to assess in a VE situation.

Practically speaking, assessment was conducted through a mixture of self-assessment in the form of weekly journals, as well as group feedback sessions during which the students worked together with other members of their own class and presented ideas and progress reports for the poster project. This had a twofold effect which allowed students to become aware of and document their own progress in the journals, as well as give us instructors the insight into how students used the target language, worked in group settings, and presented their ideas. When creating our course objectives and designing the activities, three points were chosen as assessment criteria. By modifying Byram's (1997) model for intercultural communication (see Figure 1 below), we were able to create a framework on the basis of which activities and outputs could be measured and assessed.

The first point, speaker confidence, was measured by the speech rate and utterance length as well as the length of the pauses between those utterances. In most classroom situations a confident speaker will be able to produce speech at a comfortable rate and avoid any long uncomfortable pauses between utterances. The students were asked to assess themselves multiple times throughout the weekly journals with regard to these abilities and, in addition, feedback was given after any in-class presentations or group work.

Figure 1. The crucial points for fluency assessment determined for the purposes of the course on the basis of Byram's (1997) model

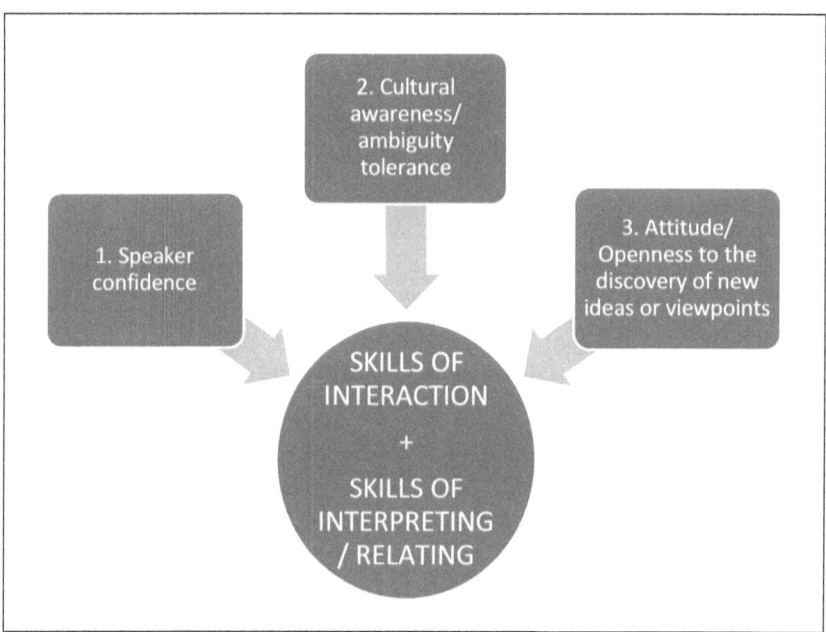

The second point (cultural awareness/ambiguity tolerance) and the third point (attitude or openness to the discovery of new viewpoints) were assessed on the basis of in-class activities, VE engagement, and self-assessment. For the students on the Bielefeld side of the VE, these two points were introduced during the first in-class meeting before the VE with partners began. The students were asked to take a communication questionnaire that was created initially for workers of international organizations in foreign countries. The questionnaire asked about students' assumptions and biases, and rated their own abilities in recognizing these ideas. Students then discussed in groups the questionnaire questions and their relevance to the course. This initial reflection activity was important for setting the tone and awakening students' awareness and sensitivity to their exchange partners. It also introduced concepts and vocabulary that the students could later use in their weekly reflection journals.

A major part of the assessment process for the Bielefeld group was the use of self-assessment in the form of a weekly journal. Each week, students were tasked with writing a reflection journal on how they felt they performed during VE sessions in terms of using the target language (the reflection prompts are included in the course syllabus in supplementary materials Appendix 1). This allowed the participants to discuss the context of the language, assess their FL use, elaborate on their own speaker confidence levels, and reflect on how they feel they came across as a communicator. A preliminary reflection journal entry was assigned to document the students' expectations of the entire experience before the VE began, whereas the final journal entry aimed to determine if those expectations were met after the sessions were completed. In this final journal entry, students were encouraged to share their hopes and fears, and to rate themselves and their abilities on the basis of a questionnaire similar to the one described before. This approach helped generate not only discussion about different ways of communicating, but also internal reflection on what determines successful communication in the VE setting.

At Cornell, their assessment was also tied to the output of the final poster project. The following criteria were provided to students as a guideline for their posters. These points were used for assessing their completed posters and were also used as the criteria for the Bielefeld group when voting for the winning posters.

> Your poster should demonstrate a clear visualization of the topic, including explanations in German. Please use the following resource on how to create a good poster – https://guides.nyu.edu/posters. Create something you would like to see. The following criteria will be considered in the evaluation:
>
> - the topic highlights a connection between Bauhaus in Germany and another country;
>
> - it is evident that you collaborated with your partner in Bielefeld;
>
> - you chose an appealing topic, e.g. a topic that is not very known;

Chapter 8

- you visualized the topic well; and

- you used Creative Commons or ensured that copyright was not violated otherwise. You can find material under a Creative Commons license here: http://search.creativecommons.org.

4. Conclusions and lessons learned

Most activities covered multiple competencies simultaneously. Just like FL speakers manage multiple speaking decisions when formulating a sentence, the same can be true for VE partners managing the cultural layer of decisions. In traditional classroom settings, as a language learner, the student is focused on the correct formation of the target language. To better prepare students for real-life communication, courses need to be designed to give multiple chances in the same activity (or related activities) for the student to realize the cultural connection embedded into the task. In VE, this can be achieved, for instance, in simple vocabulary activities, in which students 'teach' their partners key vocabulary in a topic of discussion. The use and context for this new vocabulary should be a part of this 'teaching'. We have observed many encounters within this activity that have underlined the cultural knowledge that would have otherwise gone unnoticed.

One of the main objectives of the course is to improve speaker confidence; however, this can be difficult for the instructor to assess. Confidence should be neither too low (where the participant experiences hesitation to say anything) nor too high (it may involve arrogance and possible tendency toward stereotyping and not making a personal connection with the VE partner). Using a reflective journal helped highlight the issues surrounding this factor and proved quite helpful with the Bielefeld exchange group.

Although the activities are designed to encourage discovery and discussion, the actual path to empathy and awareness differs for every student. Each student comes with a different starting point, a different background, a different opinion of the USA, and a different opinion of Germany. With our project design, we try to embrace this variety of opinions. Results from the feedback questionnaires, reflection papers, and diaries have shown evidence of a definitive shift from the use of 'us and them' to 'we'. Encouragingly we have had feedback that directly remarked how different, yet how similar, the students from the other university are to themselves. Also noteworthy is the amount of empathy and understanding that has been communicated with regard to their partners' situations in the final reflection journals. By giving learners autonomy and shifting the focus away from rigid assessment, we are able to foster cultural learning, which is closer to 'real life', and offers opportunities to grow as global citizens and experience empathy, understanding, and tolerance while collaborating.

5. Supplementary materials

https://research-publishing.box.com/s/pnyv9hxw9zo95wlawejb8wj68mn5g0f4

References

ACTFL. (2006). *Standards for foreign language learning in the 21st century* (3rd ed.). National Standards in Foreign Language Education Project.

Byram, M. (1991). Teaching culture and language towards an integrated model. In D. Buttjes & M. Byram (Eds), *Mediating languages and cultures. Towards an intercultural theory of foreign language education* (pp. 17-30). Multilingual Matters.

Byram, M. (1997). *Teaching and assessing intercultural communicative competence*. Multilingual Matters.

Furstenberg, G. (2010). A dynamic, web-based methodology for developing intercultural understanding. In *Proceedings of the 3rd International conference on intercultural collaboration* (pp. 49-58). ACM. https://doi.org/10.1145/1841853.1841861

Kramsch, C. (2011). The symbolic dimensions of the intercultural. *Language Teaching, 44*(3), 354-367. https://doi.org/10.1017/S0261444810000431

Chapter 8

Neuner, G. (1994). Fremde Welt und eigene Erfahrung - Zum Wandel der Konzepte von Landeskunde für den fremdsprachlichen Deutschunterricht. *Fremde Welt und eigene Wahrnehmung. Konzepte von Landeskunde im fremdsprachlichen Deutschunterricht. Kasseler Werkstattberichte zur Didaktik, Deutsch als Fremdsprache, 3*, 14-39.

9. Assessing intercultural learning in virtual exchange

Anastasia Izmaylova[1]

Abstract

Assessment of students' work in Virtual Exchange (VE) frequently focuses on their participation in the activities and may also include an evaluation of students' learning. In this chapter, we discuss a two-sided approach to assessing students' work in an intercultural VE project. On the one hand, we evaluated students' engagement in the exchange with the goal of formally assessing their work and assigning it a grade. On the other, we looked at students' intercultural competence development for research purposes. While we believe that it is beneficial to use a combination of assessment tools, reflective portfolios emerged as the most suitable way to assess students' participation, learning, and intercultural competence development in the VE.

Keywords: portfolio, reflection, culture learning, intercultural competence.

1. Introduction

VEs are one of the most convenient ways to enrich a Foreign Language (FL) classroom with authentic interactions with native speakers. There are many potential benefits to VEs, such as increased motivation (Lee, 2007; Vinagre, 2007), development of language skills (Belz & Kinginger, 2002; Chen & Yang, 2016; Liaw & English, 2013), and growth in intercultural competence

---

1. Grinnell College, Grinnell, Iowa, United States; izmaylova@grinnell.edu

How to cite: Izmaylova, A. (2022). Assessing intercultural learning in virtual exchange. In A. Czura & M. Dooly (Eds), *Assessing virtual exchange in foreign language courses at tertiary level* (pp. 135-146). Research-publishing.net. https://doi.org/10.14705/rpnet.2022.59.1415

(Jin, 2015; Lamy & Goodfellow, 2010; O'Dowd, 2007; Vinagre, 2016). The exchange discussed in this chapter was implemented with the goal of providing students with an opportunity to analyze their own and target cultures, as well as practice their intercultural communication skills. In the US class, this exchange also served as a site for a research study exploring, among other things, the development of intercultural competence. Given the twofold purpose of the exchange, there were two types of assessment. One was a part of students' grades in the course and focused on assessing their VE activities. The other one was a part of the research study and assessed the development of students' intercultural competence.

Assessment of students' activity in VE is frequently based on their participation (O'Dowd, 2010). In this approach, instructors set an expected number of posts, comments, or times students should contribute to a discussion and then count those instances for each student. While this approach is straightforward and may motivate students to do the work, it does not value the receptive part of the interactions (O'Dowd, 2010). In our experience, we found that some students do a lot of 'invisible' work in the exchange by reading and analyzing most of the conversations, while others complete the required posts with the least amount of effort (Izmaylova, 2017, 2022). Another type of assessment common in VE is self-assessment in the form of portfolios and reflections (Godwin-Jones, 2013; O'Dowd, 2010). Godwin-Jones (2013) posited that students' reflection on their intercultural communication experience is necessary for their understanding the significance of that experience and their learning. At the same time, some students may not be forthcoming in their reflections and others may lack life experience to be able to deeply reflect on their interactions. In our case, we combined the most commonly used assessment practices and evaluated students' work based on their participation and portfolios.

Evaluating intercultural competence is known to be a challenging endeavor (O'Dowd & Dooly, 2020) with little consensus among researchers on how it should be assessed and whether it should be assessed at all (Schulz, 2007; Sercu, 2004). Researchers agree that intercultural competence is too complex of a construct to evaluate through tests and standard types of assessment (Dervin,

2010; Schulz, 2007; Storme & Derakhshani, 2002), which is why alternative forms of assessment, such as surveys and portfolios are preferred (Byram, 1997; Dervin, 2010; Fantini, 2009). In addition, due to the complexity of the notion of intercultural competence, it is more feasible to focus on its specific components (e.g. openness to other cultures, skills of cultural comparison, etc.) instead of trying to evaluate it as a whole (Deardorff, 2009). For the purposes of the study, we first identified some commonalities among influential theories and conceptualizations of intercultural competence (Bennett, 1993; Byram, 1997; Kramsch, 1993) to identify the components to be assessed. In general terms, intercultural competence is viewed as an ability to mediate between cultures and to shift one's frame of reference, which requires an understanding of one's own culture and an ability to interpret foreign culture. Additionally, it may be important to understand what culture is in order to be able to analyze it. To assess these three constructs, we used a combination of pre- and post-exchange questionnaires, portfolios, and pre- and post-exchange interviews. The pre-exchange questionnaires and interviews aimed to understand students' backgrounds, expectations for the project, and their understanding of the concept of culture. Post-exchange questionnaires and interviews focused on students' experiences in the exchange, their overall learning, and intercultural competence development. The portfolios served a dual role – for students to reflect on their experience, and for us to formally assess their participation, as well as examine their intercultural learning.

2. Overview of the VE project

The two partners in this VE were two FL classes. On one side, there was a fourth semester Spanish class at a large US university. Fourth semester is the second course in the intermediate level sequence and is the last course required for all students to take. There were 19 students in the class. On the other side of the exchange was a third-semester English class at a higher education institution in Colombia. The Colombian students' levels of English was described by their instructor as approximately intermediate low to intermediate mid based on the American Council on the Teaching of Foreign Languages (ACTFL) scale. While there were approximately 40 Colombian students in the Facebook Group at the beginning of the exchange, only eight to ten students participated regularly. The goal of the exchange was for students in these two classes to practice intercultural communication in their native and in their respective target languages in an authentic context. In addition, students were expected to learn about their target cultures and practice explaining their own cultures to foreigners.

The project lasted eight weeks and was constructed as a many-to-many interaction in a private Facebook Group. Facebook was chosen as a medium for the exchange in order to make the interaction environment as authentic and similar to students' daily communication as possible. Each week students had to make one photo or video post in the group and write a caption for it. This original post was to be done in their native languages. Then students read posts made by their exchange partners and had to comment on at least two posts in the target language. In this manner, all conversations about the US culture were in English, while all conversations about the Colombian culture were in Spanish. Each week students had an assigned topic and guiding questions for their posts (see supplementary materials Appendix 1). In the US class, there was also a weekly in-class discussion about students' experience and learning in the exchange that week. These discussions were conducted in both Spanish and English to allow students an opportunity to express themselves however they wished. Students tended to begin the conversation in Spanish but switch to English once each discussion got more profound. At the end of the project, students wrote and turned in a portfolio of their experiences (see supplementary materials Appendix 2).

3. Assessment

There were two types of assessment in the exchange, one tied to the students' grades, and another one meant to assess the development of their intercultural competence for research purposes. While the first type is the most important one for the practitioners, the second one will also be explained to demonstrate the possibilities of assessing students' intercultural learning. It is important to note that this chapter describes the assessment of the US students only.

3.1. Assessing students' activities in the exchange

Students' work in the VE was assessed using their posts in the Facebook Group and their end-of-project portfolios. Their grades were based on the rubric below (Table 1).

Table 1. VE assessment rubric (Izmaylova, 2017, p. 269)

Criteria	Score
Student enters the required number of posts and comments timely (posts by Friday and comments [on the previous week's posts] by Wednesday each week).	3 – 2 – 1
Posts are thoughtful and include meaningful information about your life and American culture.	4 – 3 – 2 – 1
Student engages in conversations, when appropriate: • respond to your classmates or students from Colombia when they comment on your pictures; and • react to their responses to your questions.	3 – 2 – 1
Posts/comments are written/spoken in full sentences and express clear information/ideas; errors do not interfere with the meaning of the messages.	3 – 2 – 1
Comments are free from significant grammatical errors. Student demonstrates: • subject-verb and noun-adjective agreement; • correct verb conjugation; and • correct use of tense/aspect.	3 – 2 – 1
Portfolio is complete and turned in on time.	4 – 3 – 2 – 1
Total	___ / 20

The rubric consisted of several criteria, each having a scale of points to represent full or partial fulfillment of the requirements. First, students had to submit the required number of posts and comments before the deadline each week. Their contributions were also evaluated on how thoughtful and meaningful they were. The goal of this criterion was to have students think about the topic and guiding questions and produce a post that would help Colombian students learn something about US culture. The next criterion was whether students responded to comments that addressed them or their posts. In other words, students were expected to keep the interaction going and not disengage after completing their post and two comments. Finally, posts were holistically evaluated on their accuracy and comprehensibility. The last criterion for the grade was the completeness and timeliness of the portfolio, which will be discussed below.

At the beginning of the project, the instructor created a spreadsheet to keep track of each student's posts every week and to make notes on the quality of their content and language. However, as the semester went on this task proved to be rather overwhelming. While it was easy to find each student's original post, tracking their interactions in the comment sections was very time-consuming. In addition, the algorithms used by Facebook rely on the number and recency of interactions with each post instead of using a chronological order. This makes it easy to overlook the posts that received less attention. Additionally, it is harder to trace each student's contribution in a many-to-many interaction, which is why an exchange in pairs or small groups would have made this type of assessment more feasible. A different platform for the exchange or a different set up within the Facebook Group would likely have yielded a different result. Given how time-consuming and sometimes ineffective the rubric was, the instructor modified the rubric to only track the number of posts and comments made by the students each week, narrowing down this part of the assessment to pure participation.

In addition to their regular participation in the exchange, students created project portfolios, where they reflected on their experience and learning (supplementary materials Appendix 2). The portfolios served a dual purpose: they were used as part of summative assessment of students' work and as a research instrument to assess intercultural learning. Portfolios were briefly introduced in the beginning of the semester and discussed in more detail at the end of the VE. Students were instructed to include two to three interactions where they thought they grew as intercultural communicators and describe why they were meaningful to them. As described in the guidelines, those were not necessarily to be the best or most successful interactions, but rather ones where students learned something important. Students were given examples of what types of interactions to include but were encouraged to write about other instances as well. To ensure their complete freedom of expression and a deeper reflection, students were given the choice to write either in English or in Spanish. All students opted to write in English. In addition, the portfolio itself was not graded, but was a part of the overall VE grade. To receive full credit, students had to make sure it was complete (i.e. have two to three examples with reflections) and turn it in on time. The course instructor provided written comments to the portfolios, but there was no formal feedback to students regarding their participation in the exchange beyond the weekly class discussions. In this sense, the portfolios did not inform students' learning during the exchange, but they offered an opportunity for students to process their learning. It also allowed the instructor to reflect on how students viewed their interactions and take that into account when implementing VE in other classes.

3.2. Assessing intercultural competence development

As mentioned above, this VE was also a site for a research study on intercultural competence development through VE. The researcher used several data sources to qualitatively assess the changes in students' understanding of culture as a concept, their understanding of their own culture, and their understanding of the target culture (see supplementary materials Appendix 3 for a summary of data sources and each instrument). Prior to the exchange, students completed a background questionnaire and a project expectations questionnaire. Students' answers then informed the researcher's questions in the semi-structured one-on-one interviews. Similarly, after the exchange, students completed a project experience questionnaire. The researcher used the information from those questionnaires and students' portfolios in the post-project interviews.

All the data from the questionnaires, transcribed interviews, and portfolios was coded following a general interpretive qualitative analysis method (Merriam,

2009; Saldaña, 2016). The researcher looked for instances that referred to the three identified components of intercultural competence and completed several rounds of coding and subcoding as is typical for the iterative nature of qualitative research. While the complete findings of the research study are beyond the scope of this chapter (see Izmaylova, 2017, for detailed methodology and results), it is important to note that the use of questionnaires, interviews, and portfolios was appropriate and effective in assessing the development of students' intercultural competence. Our analysis showed that students developed a more nuanced understanding of the concept of culture and began viewing culture learning in an FL classroom more favorably as a result of the exchange. They also demonstrated an increased awareness of practices and perspectives of their own culture and were able to take on a critical stance toward it by attempting to analyze it from an outsider's perspective. Finally, while learning about common practices and perspectives in Colombian culture, students started connecting various bits of information on separate topics to make general observations about the target culture, which shows that participants developed their skills of discovering and interpreting cultural knowledge.

4. Conclusions and lessons learned

This chapter described a VE where two types of assessment took place, one used to assess students' participation and work in the exchange and another one assessing the development of students' intercultural competence. Depending on their goals, practitioners may choose to focus on either one or both.

Regarding participation, we have found it difficult and time-consuming to track each student's posts and assess each one of them using a rubric. Simply tracking the number of posts seemed to be an easier way to make sure they fulfill the requirements of the exchange, if that is needed. Similar to other scholars (Caluianu, 2019; Godwin-Jones, 2013; O'Dowd, 2010), we believe that one of the best ways to assess the work and learning of the students in VE is through a portfolio or a reflection paper. Either assignment can be tailored to the specific goals of the exchange. The benefit of a portfolio is that students need to include specific examples that impacted them, which ensures that they participate fully and reflect on that participation at the same time. The use of a portfolio also provides an opportunity for students to self-assess their learning, and for instructors to get evidence of students' intercultural competence. We recommend that practitioners include specific guidelines for the types of examples and reflection they want their students to provide. We also believe a detailed rubric would make the requirements transparent to the students and make it easier for the educators to assess the portfolios. In our example, portfolios were not graded as separate pieces of work, and we believe that this was not the most appropriate approach, as these portfolios demonstrated students' intercultural learning the best.

As for intercultural competence, it is a difficult construct to assess. The pre-exchange data showed that different students had very different levels of intercultural competence prior to the start of the exchange. Therefore, we cannot expect the same learning outcome or even the same experience for each student in the project, which means that we cannot set a goal of a certain level of intercultural competence. Practitioners may choose to look at each student's growth in intercultural competence by implementing the pre- and post-VE approach similar to the one described in this chapter. However, it may be too labor-intensive and time-consuming for a course project. In addition, we found that students' development was not linear as they demonstrated various stages and components of intercultural competence at the same time (Izmaylova, 2017). For these reasons, we return to our recommendation of a portfolio as the most appropriate assessment instrument. Using a portfolio, educators will be able to assess both the process (i.e. students' participation) and the product (i.e. students' analyses and reflections on their learning) of students' work in the VE. Combining it with a pre- and post-exchange questionnaire may also provide a more comprehensive picture of students' learning.

5. Supplementary materials

https://research-publishing.box.com/s/35588dz4aqx7y1i4njw1fwk9dojop76a

Chapter 9

References

Belz, J., & Kinginger, C. (2002). The cross-linguistic development of address form use in telecollaborative language learning: two case studies. *The Canadian Modern Language Review, 59*(2), 189-214. https://doi.org/10.3138/cmlr.59.2.189

Bennett, M. J. (1993). Towards ethnorelativism: a developmental model of intercultural sensitivity. In R. M. Paige (Ed.), *Education for the intercultural experience* (pp. 21-71). Intercultural Press.

Byram, M. (1997). *Teaching and assessing intercultural communicative competence*. Multilingual Matters.

Caluianu, D. (2019). When more is less: unexpected challenges and benefits of telecollaboration. In A. Turula, M. Kurek & T. Lewis (Eds), *Telecollaboration and virtual exchange across disciplines: in service of social inclusion and global citizenship* (pp. 7-13). Research-publishing.net. https://doi.org/10.14705/rpnet.2019.35.934

Chen, J. J., & Yang, S. C. (2016). Promoting cross-cultural understanding and language use in research-oriented Internet-mediated intercultural exchange. *Computer Assisted Language Learning, 29*(2), 262-288. https://doi.org/10.1080/09588221.2014.937441

Deardorff, D. K. (2009). Implementing intercultural competence assessment. In D. Deardorff (Ed.), *The SAGE handbook of intercultural competence* (pp. 477-491). Sage. https://doi.org/10.4135/9781071872987.n28

Dervin, F. (2010). Assessing intercultural competence in language learning and teaching: a critical review of current efforts in higher education. In F. Dervin & Eija Suomela-Salmi (Eds), *New approaches to assessing language and (inter-)cultural competences in higher education* (pp. 157-173). Peter Lang.

Fantini, A. (2009). Assessing intercultural competence: issues and tools. In D. K. Deardorff (Ed.), *The SAGE handbook of intercultural competence* (pp. 456-476). Sage. https://doi.org/10.4135/9781071872987.n27

Godwin-Jones, R. (2013). Integrating intercultural competence into language learning through technology. *Language Learning & Technology, 17*(2), 1-11.

Izmaylova, A. (2017). *Using social media to develop intercultural competence through telecollaboration*. Doctoral dissertation, University of Iowa. ProQuest Dissertation Publishing.

Izmaylova, A. (2022). Cultural identity and intercultural learning: individual learners' experiences in telecollaboration. In Klimanova, L. (Ed.), *Identity, multilingualism and CALL: responding to new global realities* (pp. 299-327). Equinox Publishing.

Jin, S. (2015). Using Facebook to promote Korean EFL learners' intercultural competence. *Language Learning & Technology, 19*(3), 38-51.

Kramsch, C. (1993). *Context and culture in language teaching*. Oxford University Press.

Lamy, M.-N., & Goodfellow, R. (2010). Telecollaboration and learning 2.0. In S. Guth & F. Helm (Eds), *Telecollaboration in education, volume 1: telecollaboration 2.0: languages, literacies and intercultural learning in the 21st century* (pp. 107-138). Peter Lang AG.

Lee, L. (2007). One-to-one desktop videoconferencing for developing oral skills: prospects in perspective In R. O'Dowd (Ed.), *Online intercultural exchange: an introduction for foreign language teachers* (pp. 281-291). Multilingual Matters. https://doi.org/10.21832/9781847690104-020

Liaw, M.-L., & English, K. (2013). Online and offsite: student-driven development of the Taiwan-France telecollaborative project Beyond These Walls. In M.-N. Lamy & K. Zourou (Eds), *Social networking for language education* (pp. 158-176). Palgrave Macmillan.

Merriam, S. (2009). *Qualitative research: a guide to design and implementation*. Jossey-Bass.

O'Dowd, R. (2007). *Online intercultural exchange: an introduction for foreign language teachers*. Multilingual Matters. https://doi.org/10.21832/9781847690104

O'Dowd, R. (2010). Issues in assessment of online interaction and exchange. In S. Guth & F. Helm (Eds), *Telecollaboration in education, volume 1: telecollaboration 2.0: languages, literacies and intercultural learning in the 21st century* (pp. 69-106). Peter Lang AG.

O'Dowd, R., & Dooly, M. (2020). Intercultural communicative competence through telecollaboration and Virtual Exchange. In J. Jackson (Ed.), *The Routledge handbook of language and intercultural communication* (2nd ed., pp. 361-375). Routledge. https://doi.org/10.4324/9781003036210-28

Saldaña, J. (2016). *The coding manual for qualitative researchers* (3rd ed.). SAGE Publications.

Schulz, R. A. (2007). The challenge of assessing cultural understanding in the context of foreign language instruction. *Foreign Language Annals 40*(1), 9-26. https://doi.org/10.1111/j.1944-9720.2007.tb02851.x

Sercu, L. (2004). Assessing intercultural competence: a framework for systematic test development in foreign language education and beyond. *Intercultural Education, 15*(1), 73-89. https://doi.org/10.1080/1467598042000190004

Storme, J. A., & Derakhshani, M. (2002). Defining, teaching, and evaluating cultural proficiency in the foreign language classroom. *Foreign Language Annals, 35*(6), 657-668. https://doi.org/10.1111/j.1944-9720.2002.tb01904.x

Chapter 9

Vinagre, M. (2007). Integrating tandem learning in higher education. In R. O'Dowd (Ed.), *Online intercultural exchange: an introduction for foreign language teachers* (pp. 240-249). Multilingual Matters. https://doi.org/10.21832/9781847690104-014

Vinagre, M. (2016). Promoting intercultural competence in culture and language studies: outcomes of an international collaborative project. In E. Martín-Monje, I. Elorza & B. García Riaza (Eds), *Technological advances in specialized linguistic domains: practical applications and mobility* (pp. 23-35). Routledge.

10 Business communication skills through virtual exchange – a case study

Jean-François Vuylsteke[1]

Abstract

Assessing the skills of the students who take part in a Virtual Exchange (VE) project is a challenging and complicated task, especially if it aims to engage both the students and VE co-organisers in the feedback and evaluation process. The objective of this chapter is to outline the pedagogical design of a business communication skills course and present how a VE component and its assessment were integrated into the core course syllabus. The text explains how all the members of the created VE learning community were involved in defining the skills to be developed by the students. Pedagogical choices were made that involved the design of the learning path, the design of the VE activities, and the course assessment in such a way that everyone had a precise role to play. In particular, the chapter focuses on how different assessment tools prompted the students to reflect on the development of language competence while working together to prepare for a professional job interview in an international and collaborative learning setting.

Keywords: assessment, portfolio, virtual exchange, responsibility, soft skills.

---

1. Ecole Pratique des Hautes Etudes Commerciales (EPHEC), Brussels, Belgium; jf.vuylsteke@ephec.be; https://orcid.org/0000-0003-1762-0735

How to cite: Vuylsteke, J.-F. (2022). Business communication skills through virtual exchange – a case study. In A. Czura & M. Dooly (Eds), *Assessing virtual exchange in foreign language courses at tertiary level* (pp. 147-162). Research-publishing.net. https://doi.org/10.14705/rpnet.2022.59.1416

1. Introduction

For the past 15 years, I have integrated two pedagogical pillars into my business English course at EPHEC (Ecole Pratique des Hautes Etudes Commerciales, Brussels) university college: (1) VE activities, and (2) applied case studies. However, it is only quite recently that these activities have turned digital and that, in addition to learning how to interact and cope in English in different business situations, the students also began developing their soft skills. In 2019, a VE project with the PPCU (Pázmány Péter Catholic University) in Budapest started in which students worked collaboratively in order to develop both their digital and language skills.

The business communication course design at EPHEC was supported with the *ABC Learning Design Model* (Young & Perovic, 2016; https://abc-ld.org/; Jourde & Gallenne, 2021), a curriculum development tool that helps to design new courses or adapt the existing ones to the needs of an online or blended learning format. It also calculates the time spent by all the participants on achieving the learning path designed in the course. The teaching methodology was based both on flipped classroom (cf. Awidi & Paynter, 2018; Chuang, Weng, & Chen, 2018) and the *six learning styles* approaches (Laurillard et al., 2018). The flipped classroom approach (referred to also as 'the inverted classroom', 'flipped learning', or 'the flip'; cf. Arnold-Garza, 2014, p. 8) is a pedagogical model in which students get acquainted with the learning materials (e.g. recorded lectures, articles, textbooks) before the class, whereas the classroom time is used to deepen understanding of the content through discussion and problem-solving activities. As Dooly and Sadler (2019, p. 2) underline, this approach "should be seen as placing emphasis on active learning, both inside and outside the class". The application of flipped learning in our VE project, which aimed to make it possible for students to keep learning when outside the classroom, required that the course material be adapted and tailored appropriately. That is why 100% of the course content was made available online on the Learning Management System (LMS)[2] platform of the course.

---

2. EPHEC LMS platform is Moodle. This LMS platform enables the students to get access to learning paths designed by their lecturers and made 100% available online.

Apart from the flipped classroom element, the course design made use of *six learning types*, which involve "learning through Acquisition (i.e., to read/watch/listen), Collaboration, Discussion, Investigation, Practice, and Production". This models draws from the theory-based Conversational Framework, where each type of learning activity "is a cycle between learner and teacher, or learner and peers, at the concept and/or practice level" (Laurillard, 2012 in Laurillard et al., 2018, p. 1049). Consequently, in this business English course, a large space is designated for exchange in the classroom, self-study, personal research, and peer-to-peer learning and assessment.

When a VE component was added to the original business communication course, assessment presented its own challenges and these had to be considered in the process of designing the course. How is it possible to reach a high-standard level of assessment which remains fair for all the students, knowing that much of the learning process takes place outside the classroom? How can one measure, weigh, and assess the students' learning processes when it is out of the presence of the teacher/lecturer? Thus, in the rest of chapter, the business communication course is explained, the original teaching method outlined, the VE project in the course is summarised, the business communication course objectives are explained, the learning outcomes described, and the assessment approach adopted in this VE course by the Belgian partner is laid out. In particular, attention is paid to the importance of keeping a balance between testing, peer-to-peer assessment, informative evaluation, and self-study grading.

2. Overview of the project

This 12-week-long business communication course in the Belgian institution was addressed to undergraduate students and involved an eight-week VE component. The remaining four weeks were used for in-class introduction and conclusion. The whole course was organised around the learning modules (see Figure 1), which were introduced in-class by the teacher and led to class discussions, group work, and both individual application and production exercises.

Figure 1. The business communication course content on the LMS platform

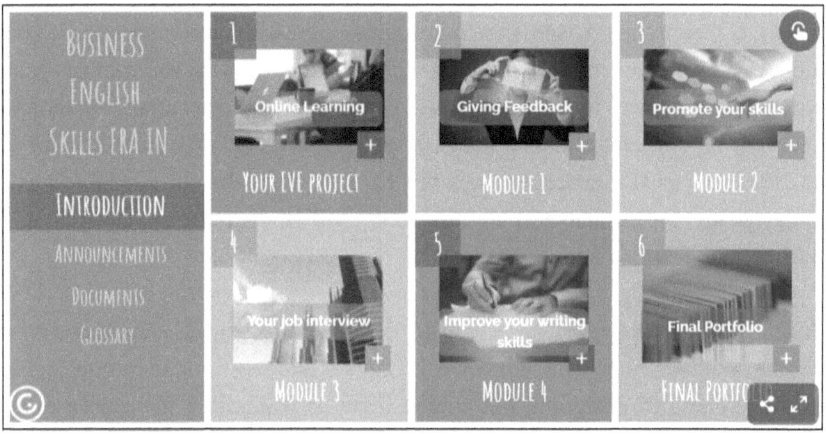

According to the *ABC Learning Design* (cf. Young & Perovic, 2016) time estimates, the whole learning process in the business communication course included:

- +/- 20 hours spent in class and in the presence of the teacher;

- +/- 40 hours of the learning time spent in asynchronous activities – the VE component included;

- +/- 10 hours spent in both formative and summative assessment of the students; and

- +/- 16 hours of the learning time spent in small teams – the VE component included.

The self-study exercises, video material, quizzes, texts, forums, vocabulary, and grammar input were easily available in the LMS platform (see Figure 2). The grammar and lexical revision exercises were completely digitalised and integrated in the learning path of the students. This solution offered the possibility of organising the necessary vocabulary and grammar activities outside the classroom. Self-study and revision activities were scheduled prior to certification quizzes made in class.

Figure 2. Interactive language-oriented tasks on Moodle platform

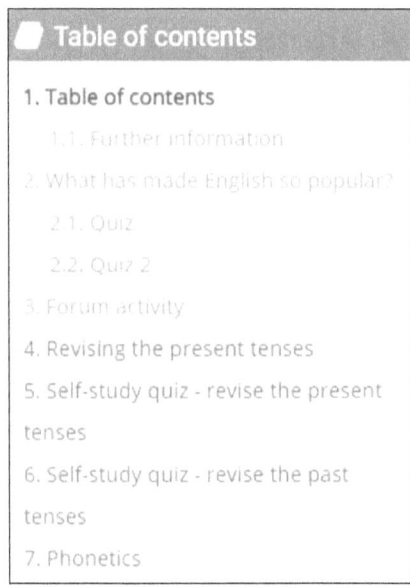

Additionally, the LMS platform provided the teacher with results and indications about the completion of each student's learning journey, including their participation in different stages of the VE project (see Figure 3). This enabled efficient feedback provision, the possibility of sending reminders and adjusting in-class activities to the students' preparations.

As a part of the course, the students were involved in a VE project between a Belgian and a Hungarian university, during which they worked online in mixed international teams of five to six students on topics and tasks introduced during in-class meetings in their home institutions. The students were given the same deadlines, instructions, and input material. The VE activities centred on five main missions and tasks: (1) giving constructive feedback, (2) creating an elevator pitch, (3) creating a digital CV, (4) preparing for a job interview, and (5) participating in a real online job interview with a professional recruiter. During weekly online synchronous sessions, the students from both institutions completed both individual and group tasks, starting from ice-breaking exercises, to more business-oriented activities that centred on navigating a job recruitment process (more detailed description of the VE component in both institutions can be found in Koris & Vuylsteke, 2020).

Figure 3. Moodle completion progress bar

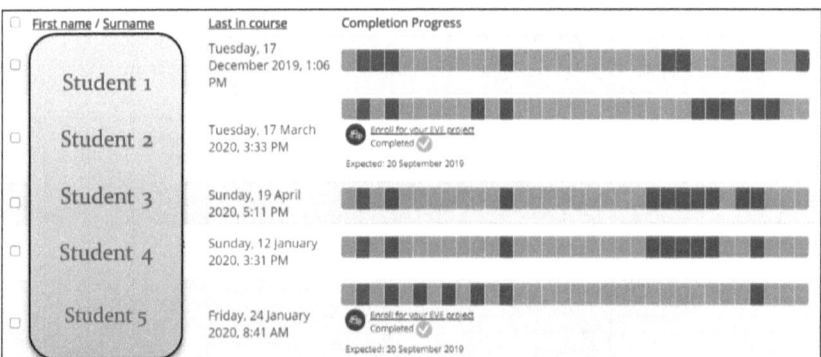

3. Assessment in the VE project

Given that the normal teaching programme is 12 weeks long, the eight-week VE project was designed to weigh significantly in the assessment. The students were told that instead of a final exam there would be a final face-to-face meeting with the teacher. The meeting would be based on their personal portfolio as support for evidence of their learning journey. Everything they were assigned to do (research, exercises, written, and oral productions, etc.) would be taken into account in the calculation of the final grade. Given the number of persons involved (two lecturers, the external recruiters, and the students), it was necessary to propose uniform assessment criteria and to follow the same assessment guidelines. Table 1 lists the Belgian students' course assignments and presents the responsibility delegated to each party involved in the assessment process in this VE project.

Table 1. Division of responsibility in the assessment process

	The Belgian teacher	The Hungarian teacher	The recruiters	The students
Self-study quizzes				Multiple attempts possible until they reach 70% of correct answers
Certification quizzes	One single attempt in class			
Forums	Feedback and grading			Feedback only
The three team reports And the team charter	Co-assessment	Co-assessment		
Other VE productions	Feedback and grading			Feedback only during the VE
Video pitch	Feedback and grading for oral production			Feedback only during the VE
Class discussions	Grading for oral production			
Presentations	Grading for oral production			Feedback via Wooclap
Digital CV	Formative feedback		Feedback	Feedback only during the VE
Web mag productions	Grading for written production			Groupwork interaction analysis
Job interview			Feedback and grading	
Final portfolio	Grading for written production			
Final face-to-face meeting	Grading for final VE and oral production			
VE return on experience				Grade awarded on the basis of collected evidence

3.1. Collaborative written reports

It was decided that all online meetings organised during the VE would result in a written group assignment: three meeting reports, a team charter, and different mind maps representing the outcomes of their discussions. This material was given feedback upon reception and systematically assessed for content, style, and grammar. Antidote 10[3], a correction software which offered the possibility for us to automatically share feedback about style and grammar, was used. All these documents contained paragraphs that had to be filled in by the teams and a final section that had to be completed individually by each team member. This allowed each VE project teacher to provide a grade for each team production but also for each student's individual contribution.

All the online meetings were recorded and shared among the team members. The objective was to always keep the results of the students' discussions available for each team member and to allow them to rewind any past recording to get information to complete their assignments and portfolios (see below).

3.2. Online magazines

In addition to this, the Belgian students were asked to coproduce two web magazines. The first one was designed together with the students from Budapest as an introductory activity aiming to break the ice and let the students introduce themselves to their potential VE partners. The second web magazine, prepared in teams by Belgian students only, contained tips and advice about how to succeed at a job interview. This collaborative contribution was submitted at the end of the VE, when all the interviews were over, and their learning journey completed. It was the students' final written team production, giving the teacher an opportunity to assess how they worked together in order to coproduce the magazine.

---

3. Antidote 10, https://www.antidote.info/en/antidote-10

3.3. The job interview

During the VE meetings, the students were involved in a number of activities that aimed to help them prepare for a realistic online job interview, coached and assessed by external professional recruiters. Before the interview, the students were expected to share their earlier output, such as elevator pitches and interactive digital CVs, with the external professional recruiters. After the interview, the students from both institutions got feedback from the recruiters, who were fully in charge of assessing this component. For this reason, both involved VE teachers proposed an assessment grid to the recruiters (see supplementary materials, Appendix 1).

3.4. Presentation

Finally, once the VE had been completed, students were asked to prepare a short presentation of what they had learnt. The presentation was recorded and shared online. It was limited in time (five minutes maximum) and in the number of slides commented by the students (five maximum). The clips were then submitted to groups of five, for feedback and comments. Wooclap[4] was used to propose the same feedback guidelines to all students taking part in the assessment. Wooclap makes it easy to aggregate the remarks and feedback of the assessing students and to propose one PDF document with the report filled in by the evaluation team, as in the examples in Figure 4.

The students got a code to access the Wooclap interface and directly provided their personal choices/answers. We had agreed on an assessment grid which was then transferred to the Wooclap system. At the end of each presentation, the teacher's and the students' feedback was discussed and compared to formulate suggestions and give each student guidelines about making better presentations.

---

4. Wooclap https://www.wooclap.com/

Figure 4. Screenshots of peer feedback via Wooclap

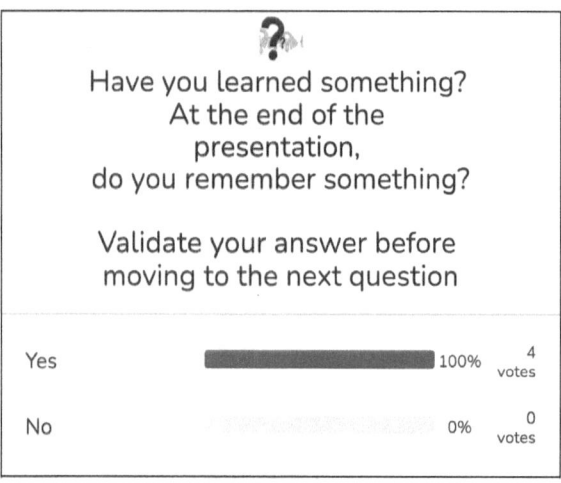

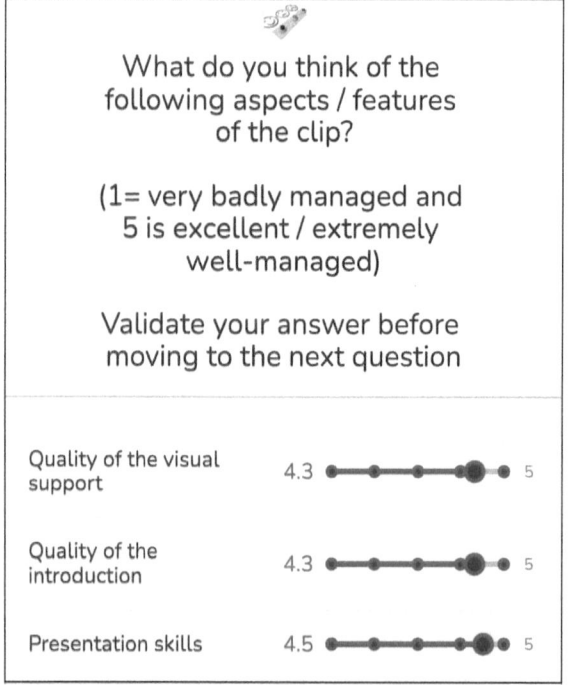

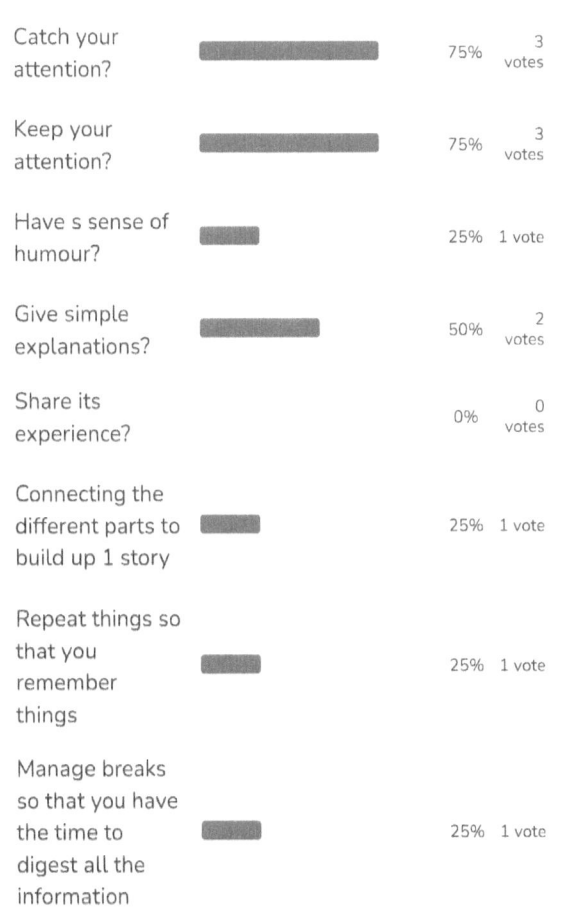

3.5. The final portfolio

The introduction of a digital portfolio was a crucial element in the strategy developed by the teachers in both participating institutions. The objective was that the students (from EPHEC and PPCU) could keep a trace of everything they have done, learnt, searched, and produced, not only in the course of the VE but also throughout the programme, and present it as evidence of their learning outcomes in the final feedback session with the teacher. In particular, the students were asked to keep a record of "the successful completion of their assignments, document the professional and soft skills they had developed, the challenges they had faced, and provide examples for their intercultural learning" (Koris & Vuylsteke, 2020, p. 72).

3.6. Face-to-face meeting

The final face-to-face meeting of Belgian students with their teacher was looked upon as an important step in the global assessment of the students' acquired business skills by the end of the term. During this meeting, on the basis of the evidence collected in the portfolio, i.e. the grades they collected for all the self-study quizzes they had completed, the feedback given by their teammates during the VE, their vision of their personal level of proficiency at the end of the VE, the students could propose their final grade.

3.7. In-class versus VE assessment

Their ability to communicate in English was also measured when grading their oral and written productions in class. The quizzes were there to help individualise the assessment and counterbalance the weight of the team production in their evaluation. The teacher could also assess how they performed in English in different situations (e.g. online meetings) while coaching the production of the second web mag (the one they produced in teams). It provided evidence of how they excelled in promoting their skills when taking a realistic job interview, grading their pitches, and receiving the external recruiters' final assessments.

This is the reason why the students' individual and team grades were given the below weight in the calculation of their final grades.

- Sixty percent of the final grade for all the class and VE activities related to the course modules including: (1) the grammar/vocabulary and other quizzes; (2) the individual and team productions, web magazines; and (3) the oral activities and the animated feedback session, presentations included.

- Forty percent for the outputs of the in-class and VE activities including: (1) the VE self-assessment by the students; (2) the final portfolio; (3) the final face-to-face; and (4) the job interviews.

4. Conclusions and lessons learnt

Involving students in their assessment process is a first step in empowering them to measure the efforts they make to reach their objectives. It is giving them the responsibility of co-assessing everything they do when working outside the classroom and providing their teammates with the most constructive feedback – not only about the hard skills they acquire, but also about the related soft skills. From the start the teacher was open to trying an assessment system in which each learning partner could contribute. These encompassed the VE partner from Budapest (for the activities in relation to the VE) but also the recruiters (for the job interview) and the students (providing peer-to-peer assessment and feedback in class from time to time). Knowing who is in charge of the grading is one thing, combining all of them in the calculation of the final grade is another challenge. That is why prioritisation is so important and must be based on the learning outcomes set for the course at the beginning of the year.

The adopted approach to assessment afforded the students the opportunity to contribute to their assessment, for instance by encouraging self-reflection, which proved truly effective. Most of the students had been able to evaluate their skills in an adequate way. In +/-30% of the cases, the awarded percentage was a bit underestimated, with a difference of one to 1.5 points out of 20. For one student out of two, the mark totally corresponded to the one the teacher would have awarded (taking all the grades collected into account). Only two students out of ten overestimated themselves. In these cases, a few aspects were missing from their considerations, and the analysis lacked depth and did not meet the satisfaction requirements. It was the first time that such a high percentage of the feedback would be given by students to other students (sharing their first impressions, quoting positive elements, and making suggestions to improve less convincing points). This was possible because they were all trained to give professional feedback and they were expected to regularly do so.

Without a doubt, this approach can be questioned and improved. For instance, it is worth considering how to provide a larger space for self-assessment and how to better include it in the grading system. The teacher aimed to challenge the students on giving their feedback about how they managed teamwork (based on the way they had managed the team production of their second web magazine) and from this some issues emerged. For instance, to provide feedback on the teamwork management, the *Team_effectiveness_questionnaire* (University of Colorado, n.d.) was used to create an Excel document which was very helpful to animate a group discussion; however, unfortunately it was not tailored to give a mark based on the students' collective conclusions.

A Moodle app called Dynamo is in preparation and should enable students to assess their own and the other students' commitment in teamwork. What is special about this app is that students would be asked questions about the way the team worked together, and make it possible to spot inactive students, unproductive followers, authoritative leaders, and so on. It would allow students to compare satisfaction scores they award to themselves and to their teammates. In addition, an algorithm would calculate each student's degree of commitment in the completion of the team activity. The teacher in charge can be free to integrate this percentage in the calculation of the final grade for this team activity and moderate it individually according to the scores obtained. This would be yet another tool that would help involve the students in the evaluation of their own skills.

As a final thought, if I were to have more time in class, I would also try to invite the students to fill in a satisfaction chart at the end of the most relevant oral or written assignments (see supplementary materials Appendix 2 for examples). This would give the students the opportunity to analyse his/her production according to criteria listed in a grid and, ideally, open a constructive dialogue with the lecturer on the basis of a radar graph that automatically shows the points of convergence.

5. Acknowledgements

The "Developing one's business communication skills through virtual exchange" was given the European Language Label Award by the Belgian Minister-President of the Wallonia Brussels Federation and EU Commissary for Innovation, Research, Culture, Education and Youth on April 28, 2021.

6. Supplementary materials

https://research-publishing.box.com/s/xweoa5egmtkho6weq6i7uatbqkt5wphi

Recommended readings

- https://www.enseigner.ulaval.ca/guide-web/guide-des-bonnes-pratiques-de-l-enseignement-en-ligne#categorie-16
- https://teaching.cornell.edu/spring-teaching-resources/assessment-evaluation/peer-assessment
- https://www.uantwerpen.be/en/centres/centre-expertise-higher-education/didactic-information/teaching-tips-english/assessing-students/pa-reliability/
- https://abc-ld.org/
- https://abc-ld.org/6-learning-types/

Chapter 10

References

Arnold-Garza, S. (2014). The flipped classroom teaching model and its use for information literacy instruction. *Communications in Information Literacy, 8*(1), 7-22. https://doi.org/10.15760/comminfolit.2014.8.1.161

Awidi, I. T., & Paynter, M. (2018). The impact of a flipped classroom approach on student learning experience. *Computers & Education, 128*, 269-283. https://doi.org/10.1016/j.compedu.2018.09.013

Chuang, H.-H., Weng, C.-Y., & Chen, C.-H. (2018). Which students benefit most from a flipped classroom approach to language learning? Flipped classroom does not fit all students. *British Journal of Educational Technology, 49*(1), 56-68. https://doi.org/10.1111/bjet.12530

Dooly, M., & Sadler, R. (2019). "If you don't improve, what's the point?" Investigating the impact of a "flipped" online exchange in teacher education. *ReCALL, 32*(1), 4-24. https://doi.org/10.1017/S0958344019000107

Jourde, F., & Gallenne, E. (2021). *ABC Learning designer*. https://sites.google.com/view/learning-designer-spreadsheet/

Koris, R., & Vuylsteke, J.-F. (2020). Mission (im)possible: developing students' international online business communication skills through virtual teamwork. In F. Helm & A. Beaven (Eds), *Designing and implementing virtual exchange – a collection of case studies* (pp. 69-79). Research-publishing.net. https://doi.org/10.14705/rpnet.2020.45.1116

Laurillard, D. (2012). *Teaching as a design science*. Routledge.

Laurillard, D., Kennedy, E., Charlton, P., Wild, J., & Dimakopoulos, D. (2018). Using technology to develop teachers as designers of TEL: evaluating the learning designer. *British Journal of Educational Technology, 49*(6), 1044-1058. https://doi.org/10.1111/bjet.12697

University of Colorado. (n.d.). *The team effectiveness diagnostic*. https://www.cu.edu/sites/default/files/Team_effectiveness_questionnaire.pdf

Young, C., & Perovic, N. (2016). Rapid and creative course design: as easy as ABC? *Procedia - Social and Behavioral Sciences, 228*, 390-395.

11. Assessment in the English for Academic Study Telecollaboration (EAST) project – a case study

Anna Rolińska[1] and Anna Czura[2]

Abstract

This case study presents and discusses the English for Academic Study Telecollaboration (EAST) project, carried out between Science, Engineering, and Technology (SET) students from different higher education institutions. In this telecollaborative project, the students work across borders and cultures on real-life SET discipline-specific scenarios and develop a number of soft skills and attributes alongside. The paper shows how the telecollaborative exchange has been set up and what changes were required to adapt the existing course, particularly its assessment procedures, to ensure the project was well integrated into the curriculum. It also attempts to evaluate the project, taking into account the differing outcomes and learning experiences of the participants from the partnering institutions. It concludes that adding the telecollaborative project to the existing course resulted in a richer educational experience for the participants and development of a number of skills but points out imbalances in the treatment of the participants from the assessment point of view and suggests how these inequalities could be addressed in the future.

Keywords: assessment, English for academic specific purposes, telecollaboration, virtual exchange (VE).

---

1. Glasgow School of Art, Glasgow, Scotland; annarolinska@yahoo.co.uk; https://orcid.org/0000-0001-9378-1616

2. Universitat Autònoma de Barcelona, Barcelona, Spain; anna.czura@uwr.edu.pl; https://orcid.org/0000-0001-5234-6618

How to cite: Rolińska, A., & Czura, A. (2022). Assessment in the English for Academic Study Telecollaboration (EAST) project – a case study. In A. Czura & M. Dooly (Eds), *Assessing virtual exchange in foreign language courses at tertiary level* (pp. 163-175). Research-publishing.net. https://doi.org/10.14705/rpnet.2022.59.1417

Chapter 11

1. Introduction

The EAST project refers to a series of collaborative projects during the years 2015-2019. It connected international students studying on a SET strand of summer pre-sessional courses organised by the English for Academic Studies Unit at the University of Glasgow (UoG), and students enrolled in the same disciplines at the Islamic University of Gaza (IUG) (and in years 2018 and 2019 also from three other partnering institutions)[3]. In terms of student numbers, the 2015 pilot saw 37 Glasgow-based students (originally from China, Indonesia, Saudi Arabia, and Brazil) working for five weeks in August with 20 students from Gaza. The project grew exponentially over the years as the Glasgow course continued to attract higher numbers, with 140 students in 2018 and 171 in 2019. In regard to Gaza students, 52 joined in 2018 and 25 in 2019 (see Guariento, 2019, for exact details of the iterations 2015-2018). As mentioned above, in the last two years the collaboration extended to include two universities from Chile and one from Malawi (student data no longer accessible).

The project leaders at UoG (including the first author of this paper) and IUG remained the same throughout the years, which enabled them to fine-tune the collaboration in its subsequent iterations, improving for example on its technological and logistical aspects. For instance, they were constantly looking for more effective videoconferencing tools to help the students link with each other as well as facilitate the final presentations; there was also an increased recognition of the necessity to familiarise the UoG students with the Gazan context and give them and their partners time to bond with each other. At UoG, the course was taught by a varying number of English for Specific Academic Purposes (ESAP) teachers; the core idea behind the project, however, remained the same throughout the years. This can be

---

3. For the sake of clarity, it is important to note and remember the difference between the EAST project (often referred to as 'project') and the pre-sessional course (often referred to as 'course'). While the former was embedded in the latter, they are not synonymous, and theoretically speaking any student could complete the course without engaging in the project. Another thing to note is that while at the end of the project four different overseas institutions were engaged in the collaboration with UoG, the main partner right from the beginning was IUG and that is why it is given prominence in this paper.

summarised as the students collaborating across the borders to understand and analyse responses to real-life problems related to SET disciplines in the Global South.

The motivation to start the project was to equip ESAP students with skills necessary to communicate online in the globalised and rapidly changing world with people of different educational and professional cultures (cf. Lucena, Downey, Jesiek, & Elber, 2008; White, 2007). Engineering educators point to the need to develop in students "an ability to collaborate in distributed corporate settings, across countries, continents and cultures" (Schaefer et al., 2012, p. 394). This entails the need to implement concrete changes in professional training – modern universities should aim not only at developing students' theoretical knowledge, but also help them become lifelong learners and global citizens (Biggs & Tang, 2007). To this end, apart from developing communicative skills in the English language, the implementation of telecollaboration aimed to provide the students with a platform to improve their digital literacies, practise negotiation skills, and solve authentic discipline-related problems with peers from other professional, cultural, and linguistic backgrounds. Completing tasks collaboratively and cross-culturally essentially requires specific skills from students, such as the ability to engage in critical thinking, give and accept feedback, learn autonomously, and embrace ambiguity. For this reason, the course assessment included both summative and formative elements, which enabled the project leader from UoG to meet the institutional assessment-related requirements and to support the students throughout the process at the same time.

However, the students from the partnering institutions were not subject to the same assessment procedures and that imbalance was dictated by the wider context of the pre-sessional course into which the project was embedded, and the differing roles the students took on. This chapter presents how the summative and formative assessment tools in an existing course in the UK institution were adjusted to make it possible to embed the online, cross-national project into the course activities. Additionally, the role of the Gazan students as e-tutors in the assessment process will be presented and discussed.

2. Overview of the virtual exchange project

To discuss the assessment aspects of the EAST project at UoG, it is important to understand the gatekeeping function of the pre-sessional course during which the telecollaborative exchanges took place. In simple terms, the raison d'être of any pre-sessional course is to assess the international student's readiness to progress onto their postgraduate course at a UK university. This means that passing a pre-sessional course is often interpreted by admissions departments as proof of meeting the requirements of a government-accepted Secure English Language Test, such as IELTS (International English Language Testing System examination). Consequently, the pre-sessional course becomes a high stakes course that plays a decisive role in the admission process.

In relation to the EAST project, the UK-based groups consisted of international students (mostly from South East Asia and Arabic countries) who chose to complete pre-sessional ESAP, which targeted language, study skills, and subject-related content to prepare the students for their forthcoming postgraduate studies. The telecollaborative project was implemented within the existing course and had to comply with its syllabus and assessment requirements.

For the Gazan students, the participation in the EAST project was an extracurricular activity. Most of the IUG students were postgraduate students of engineering and related disciplines. The project was conducted during their summer holidays and was offered on a voluntary basis. The rationale behind the project was to help the students develop English language skills (in particular practical skills in communication, negotiation, and problem solving), digital skills, and literacies. Even though student involvement in the EAST project did not entail receiving any extra credit, it was promoted as an opportunity to cooperate in an engineering project in an international setting in English in order to strengthen their applications for prospective jobs and research grants or schemes. That was deemed as an important incentive as the unemployment rate among graduates in Palestine, particularly in the Gaza Strip, remains very high (see 'Recommended reading' for details but also a press release from the Palestinian Central Bureau of Statistics[4]). It was hoped that participating in an online telecollaborative exchange would help the students improve their prospects on the job market, including online and remote work settings beyond the Palestinian borders. What is more, the Gazan students with the experience of EAST participation stood a better chance when applying for a mobility in the subsequent years[5], which proves that the consequences of a telecollaborative project can reach far beyond the participating classrooms.

The online student meetings were devoted to discussing an engineering problem indicated as particularly pressing by the Gazan students in their region. The sample problems involved, for instance, 'development of Arabic OCR (Optical Character Recognition) technologies', 'climate change adaptation and disaster risk management for a sustainable environment', or 'waste management'. What is important, these were genuine problems that affected real people. Being faced with a discipline-specific problem occurring in an unfamiliar context forced the students to be quite innovative and analytical in devising solutions due to the politically, economically, and socially challenging context in which Gaza finds itself. The UoG students were working together, researching that problem, trying to understand it and how it affects Palestine, whereas the IUG students served as a sounding board – they responded to the ideas and tried to direct their partners' research and literature review. Participating in the exchange provided them with an invaluable opportunity to make their voice heard, which served as an additional motivator.

The telecollaborative component was an integral part of the five-week pre-sessional course and moreover was one of the threads woven into the course syllabus. It provided the basis for the research and writing project but the UK-based students had additional classes focusing on other content, knowledge, and skills. The students were expected to carry out the project mostly in their own

---

4. https://www.pcbs.gov.ps/post.aspx?lang=en&ItemID=4026

5. Due to its involvement in EAST, UoG was able to secure a total of 585,150 euro from the Erasmus International Credit Mobility Scheme, as a result of which eight Gazan students were able to undertake study at UoG in 2018 (https://www.gla.ac.uk/colleges/arts/aboutus/news/artsarchive/2018/headline_571817_en.html).

time and they worked in groups consisting of four to six, including one or two members from Gaza. They were asked to use technologies of their preference in order to maintain contact with each other. In terms of formally set up points of contact, there was an introductory session explaining the Gazan context and the rationale for the project in Week 1, and streamed presentations and a celebratory party in Week 5. The project leaders experimented with different formats in subsequent years; for example, in Year 2 they started timetabling an afternoon in Week 1 when the students were asked to establish real time video contact with each other and were offered technical support to help them navigate video conferencing software. This was dictated by the belief that time needs to be made to help students form working relationships. In the last couple of years, some of the past students tuned into the introductory session via video conference in order to tell the students about the experience and give tips on how to overcome challenges in technology, communication, and time management. Other than those sessions, the students were responsible for maintaining contact with each other. There was also a Facebook group which was facilitated by the project leaders to help the students keep on track, outlining what should be accomplished each week. The UK-based students also shared their experiences with the local project leaders so that in case of sustained lack of contact from the Gazan partners (for various reasons, individual students did drop out each summer), some interventions could be undertaken.

3. Assessment

Customarily, the UoG pre-sessional students have to submit summatively assessed work which, if passed, would open the gates for them onto the prospective postgraduate courses. In pre-EAST times, it used to be a 1,500-word written academic report researching a discipline-specific problem selected by the student and an accompanying oral presentation on the same topic. Such tasks created better opportunities for students to think more critically and more analytically. Additionally, formative feedback provided by the teachers on the first drafts of the reports helped students finalise the task.

With the introduction of EAST, the format of the summative assessment had to remain relatively unchanged to include both oral and written student output. Again, the UK-based students were supposed to write an academic report on an engineering problem and then summarise it during an oral presentation; however, this time the specific discipline-related topic that constituted the basis of the subsequent written and oral assignment was devised by the Gazan partners. Although the UK-based students worked in groups, each member had to prepare an individual written report. Gazan students would provide mentoring and feedback when it came to the subject-specific content of the reports, especially during the initial stages of the research process. For example, the UK-based students could discuss their report outlines as well as parts of the first drafts with their IUG colleagues but those discussions were concerned with the content, for example, whether a proposed solution was feasible in the Gazan context. The writing students also received formative feedback from their ESAP teachers at UoG which focused more on the language, academic style, and organisation.

There was still a presentation at the end of the course but, unlike before, it was delivered in groups, including the Gazan partner who was responsible for outlining the background to the scenario. Because of the involvement of the overseas partners, the presentations were streamed first via video conference software and then via Facebook in order to allow both parties to meet in real time. Apart from contributing to the presentation, the Gazan students would also ask questions and provide comments on the feasibility of the solutions suggested by their Glasgow-based colleagues.

As the course was taught and assessed by ESAP teachers, the assessment criteria were predominately language-oriented, e.g. language use, style, and appropriateness. As regards the content and form, the teachers also paid attention to task achievement, organisation and the use of sources, and interaction with the audience during presentations. They provided formative and summative feedback via a bespoke feedback form with the criteria listed and descriptive grades: needs work, on track, strong. This was because there was also coursework taken into account when awarding the final grade and we did not want the students to falsely believe that the grade for the presentation is the final grade for speaking, for example. The feedback form featured a box for a commentary too, in which the marker could provide more detail about what is being done well and what could be improved. There was a strong push for developmental feedback and feedforward. Each year the project leaders offered standardisation sessions to ensure parity in the feedback provided as well as fairness in grading.

For the Gazan partners, the assessment design was different and closely related to the role that they were taking on during the telecollaborative exchange as well as their unique context. Their main task was to devise a highly contextualised scenario related to SET, which included an overview of the local problem as well as the presentation of the political, economic, social and environmental issues in the region, and provide constructive content-related feedback to their partners in the UK. In other words, their role was to act as mentors or e-tutors, which was different from telecollaboration based on equal partnering and was deemed more likely to result in effective peer exchanges.

With this mentoring role in mind, the UoG designed a constructive feedback course[6] which focused on the knowledge and skills that are prerequisite for the mentoring role, such as giving effective feedback that is specific, timely, developmental, and polite. As part of that course, the Gazan students discussed the significance and principles of constructive feedback and after evaluating samples of feedback, they applied the knowledge and skills by writing up formative feedback on a sample of writing, on which they then received formative feedback from the project leaders (for details cf. Guariento, Rolińska, & Al-Masri, 2018; Rolińska & Guariento, 2017). This was not only to help them develop their understanding of their role and support their Glasgow-based counterparts efficiently and effectively, but it was also meant to help them develop a number of soft skills, such as teamwork, communication, problem solving, etc. to strengthen their position when applying for online and/or international jobs and, in the long turn, address the issue of youth unemployment on the domestic market within Gaza. Based on the feedback from the participating students, the constructive feedback course was effective and let the Gazan students develop

---

6. The course is an open-access resource under CC licence accessible at https://goo.gl/ifxdh7.

a number of skills. Self-selected individuals wrote reflections on the topic, with one of them providing an elaborate analysis of how the mentoring training and experience during the EAST allowed her to hone in on her teaching skills (see Rolińska, Guariento, Abouda, & Nakprada, 2020 for details).

But at the end of the day, it has to be pointed out, the project leaders were unable to offer any assessment procedure that would give the Gazan students what the UK partners were getting – an open door to the next step of study or at least some form of validation of their learning. In one of the iterations of the project, in 2016, thanks to the ELTRA (English Language Teaching Research Awards) funding from the British Council, teaching assistants from the relevant graduate school were hired to provide content feedback on presentations and short reports delivered by Gazan students. However, without the funding from an external body, there were insufficient resources to repeat this in the subsequent years. Also for reasons related to quality assurance, the project leaders were not even able to offer an official certificate of project completion – instead an informal certificate of participation was sent to the Gazan students by post.

4. Conclusions and lessons learnt

In regard to the quality of student engagement and outputs, the project leaders' observations seemed to be pointing to analytically stronger assignments, which translated into higher final grades, as compared to the results obtained by students in earlier courses before telecollaboration had been introduced. The telecollaborative component could have been a contributing factor – some students reported on feeling more motivated to read more widely and think more deeply as they were dealing with genuine problems. The same stood for the presentation which in the previous years had had to be delivered individually, whereas with the EAST project it was a group effort. Because of the collaborative aspect, apart from the content knowledge, the students were getting more informal opportunities for practising spoken English, as well as teamwork, task and time management, negotiating, problem solving, and a wealth of other soft skills, which are all competencies and attributes sought after by prospective employers. The results of a student survey conducted after the completion of the EAST project indicate that the students found this experience as "particularly gratifying in terms of general academic development and cross-cultural awareness, but also clear as regards problem-solving and teamwork" (Rolińska, Guariento, & Al-Masri, 2017, p. 35). Even though the UK-based students worked on solving the same problem in groups, their individual reports and presentations offered different insights, depending on each student's field of expertise – a computer scientist and a statistician naturally would have a different take on the problem of devising Arabic OCR software and would look into different solutions.

In summary, despite an increased workload due to logistics of the project, e.g. having to stay in touch with partners in Gaza, organising group work, and looking for sources in English on under-researched topics, the telecollaborative exchange proved to be a success. This was mainly because the pre-sessional students from the UoG were tasked with researching an authentic SET problem, which went 'beyond the textbook', as one student articulated the benefit of being involved in the project in the post-project survey. In other words, from the students' point of view, EAST meant an enriched syllabus involving content-based discussions and assessment design which catered for *assessment OF learning* but also and more importantly *assessment FOR learning*. This enrichment was possible due to the fact that the students received formative feedback on their written reports from their ESAP teachers (to ensure they were developing their language skills, and they were fairly graded at the end of the course) as well as their Gazan mentors (to warrant that the solutions and responses they offered in their reports were relevant and realistic).

The imbalance in the assessment procedures in the partner institutions resulted in unequal commitment and involvement on the part of some students. The participation of the Gazan students in the EAST project was voluntary and based on good will, particularly as the project took place during a summer holiday time. Some of the students from the partnering institution were participating less actively or even dropped out half way through the project and that was factored into the project design. Different assessment and feedback mechanisms were interwoven into the project in response to differing needs of the partners and, unfortunately, also reflecting the context and the imbalance of power between the Global South and North (please refer to further reading for more detail, especially Guariento, 2020). Ideally, both sets of students would be getting comparable teaching and learning in the form of the learning outcomes. The project leaders envisage that a telecollaborative project between international students already on their postgraduate courses and their counterparts in other countries, with oversight from both language and content specialists for the whole cohort, and credit in recognition of the participation would be most effective. Pairing up such a credit-bearing telecollaborative course with a showcase of projects to prospective employers would be another step forward in levelling up opportunities for students from the Global South and North.

The project leaders are aware that even though the students are engaged in a task involving content subject knowledge, the assessment criteria do not necessarily promote engagement with knowledge as the language teachers sometimes do not possess adequate discipline-related expertise. It needs to be pointed out, however, that the EAST project takes place as a part of ESAP course that aims not as much at developing students' content knowledge as at preparing students to undertake a postgraduate course in English in terms of communicative skills, study skills, and subject-specific language skills that would enable the students to pursue postgraduate studies in their chosen field. The objectives of the EAST project are consonant with what the project teachers value in language education – it is more about lifelong learning and developing as a reflective learner, and becoming an analytical, critical, and creative thinker.

Recommended readings

Project website: www.easttelecollaboration.wordpress.com

Guariento, B. (2019). Four years of Glasgow-Gaza pre-sessional English telecollaboration: reflections from an ethical perspective. In A. Phipps, N. Al-Masri, & G. Fassetta (Eds), *"Can you hear me?" Engaging multilingually in online international academic collaborations when borders are impassable.* Multilingual Matters.

Guariento, B., Al-Masri, N., & Rolinska, A. (2016) Investigating EAST (A Scotland-Gaza English for academic study telecollaboration between SET students). *American Society for Engineering Education 123rd Annual Conference Proceedings, New Orleans, USA*.

Rolińska, A., Guariento, B., Abouda, G., & Nakprada, O. (2020). 'Really Talking' to Gaza: from active to transformative learning in distributed environments and under highly pressured conditions. In G. Fassetta, N. Al-Masri & A. Phipps (Eds), *Multilingual online academic collaborations as resistance: crossing impassable borders* (pp. 94-115). Multilingual Matters.

References

Biggs, J., & Tang, C. (2007). *Teaching for quality learning at university* (3rd ed.). SRHE and Open University Press.

Guariento, B. (2019). Four years of Glasgow-Gaza pre-sessional English telecollaboration: reflections from an ethical perspective. In A. Phipps, N. Al-Masri, & G. Fassetta (Eds), *"Can you hear me?" Engaging multilingually in online international academic collaborations when borders are impassable*. Multilingual Matters.

Guariento, B. (2020). Pre-sessional English language courses: university telecollaboration as a driver of Global North / South student-contact for engineers [Blog post]. EAP for Social Justice. 6 June 2020. https://eap4socialjustice.net/2020/06/06/pre-sessional-english-language-courses-university-telecollaboration-as-a-driver-of-global-north-south-student-contact-for-engineers/

Guariento, W., Rolińska, A., & Al-Masri, N. (2018). Constructive content-based feedback in EAP contexts: lessons from a cross-border engineering-related pre-sessional course. *Higher Education Research & Development, 37*(3), 514-532. https://doi.org/10.1080/07294360.2018.1430124

Lucena, J., Downey, G., Jesiek, B., & Elber, S. (2008). Competencies beyond countries: the re-organization of engineering education in the United States, Europe and Latin America. *Journal of Engineering Education, 97*(4), 433-447. https://doi.org/10.1002/j.2168-9830.2008.tb00991.x

Rolińska, A., & Guariento, B. (2017) *Constructive feedback course*. University of Glasgow. https://easttelecollaboration.wordpress.com/project-media/constructive-feedback-course/

Rolińska, A., Guariento, B., Abouda, G., & Nakprada, O. (2020). 'Really Talking' to Gaza: from active to transformative learning in distributed environments and under highly pressured conditions. In G. Fassetta, N. Al-Masri & A. Phipps (Eds), *Multilingual online academic collaborations as resistance: crossing impassable borders* (pp. 94-115). Multilingual Matters.

Rolińska, A., Guariento, B., & Al-Masri, N. (2017). *English for specific academic purposes student partnerships across borders.* British Council English Language Teaching Research Paper.

Schaefer, D., Panchal, J. H., Thames, J. L., Haroon, S., & Mistree, F. (2012). Innovative design education in a global distance learning setting. *International Journal of Engineering Education, 28*(2), 381-396.

White, C. (2007). Focus on the language learner in an era of globalization: tensions, positions and practices in technology-mediated language teaching. *Language Teaching, 40*(4), 321-326. https://doi.org/10.1017/S026144480700451X

Author index

A
Aranha, Solange v, 6, 65

C
Cavalari, Suzi Marques Spatti vi, 6, 65
Czura, Anna v, 1, 5, 7, 8, 29, 47, 93, 163

D
Dolcini, Grace vi, 7, 123
Dooly, Melinda v, 1, 5, 7, 13, 47, 107

E
Elstermann, Anna-Katharina vi, 6, 79

I
Izmaylova, Anastasia vi, 8, 135

M
Matthias Phelps, Grit vii, 7, 123

R
Rolińska, Anna vii, 8, 163

S
Sendur, Agnieszka M. vii, 7, 93

V
Vuylsteke, Jean-François vii, 8, 147

www.ingramcontent.com/pod-product-compliance
Lightning Source LLC
Chambersburg PA
CBHW022010160426
43197CB00007B/364